Beyond the Blackboard

Lessons on Love from the School With No Name.

Stacey Bess

D0095906

Bess, Stacey
Beyond the Blackboard (softbound edition) previously published as Nobody
Don't Love Nobody: Lessons on Love from the School With No Name /
by Stacey Bess.
p. cm.
ISBN 978-0-61547309-3
1. Homeless students--Utah--Salt Lake City--Case studies.
2. School With No Name (Salt Lake City, Utah) II. Title

Printed in the United States of America
Design by Byron G. Warner
Photography by Rick Egan

In order to preserve the privacy of my students, some events have been
altered as to time and place, and the characters presented in this book are
composites. Also, I wish to thank the teachers who shared with me the
various lessons presented in this book. They were told to me word of mouth,
and I take no credit for their origination.

WITH LOVE. . .

To my husband, Gregory. Thank you for your incredible examples of love, patience, and sacrifice. Without your support, this important work would not have been done.

To Nichole, my oldest child. Thank you for your unending sacrifice in behalf of those children who are less fortunate.

To Brandon. Your tenderness, snuggles, and understanding have helped me along the way. Thank you.

To McKenzie Anne, my princess, for your gifts of love to me and to the children.

To Jason. You keep my life filled with laughter and remind me of the value of the phrase I Love You.

To Gavin. I am amazed at the depth of love I have for your sense of justice and your kind heart. Anyone would be lucky to be your friend.

To Garrett. My little caboose! You are a gift straight from heaven. Those beautiful eyes and smile make all my worries fade away.

I could not do what I do without the amazing sacrifice and love from my children and husband.

Contents

..........Acknowledgments viii

..........Introduction ix

1........Toughen Up and Teach Them................................3

2........What Happens to the Promise?.............................13

3........The Giving Is Enough 29

4........"Don't Be a Kid" Rules 47

5........What Dana Gave 67

6........All That Can Be Yours 81

7........Blowin' Sugar 99

8........Where Is My Mom?...125

9........Hungry Eyes..145

10.....Now Josh, They're Waiting..................................163

11.....McKenzie's Gift of Love 173

12.....The Greatest Love of All...................................183

13.....The Adult Homeless Population:
The Unhealed Child 205

..........A Simple Answer to a Complex Problem: Serve.....219

☜ ACKNOWLEDGMENTS ✂

My heartfelt thanks for help with this project goes out to . . .

Paul Rawlins, my editor at Gold Leaf Press, who has stuck by me for almost a year now. Thank you for being my partner in sharing these lessons in love. It took your writing talent to make this book work. You helped me throughout to say things the way they needed to be said in order to touch the heart.

Stephanie Burnett, who insisted that these stories contained lessons we needed to learn as a society and that I owed it to my students. She never abandoned me along the way, while she read and reread, typed, and, most importantly, made sure that I stayed true to the people.

The Salt Lake City School District Administration and Sally Lafferty in particular for understanding that my passion and what must have become tiresome requests were in behalf of the children.

The many volunteers, especially the students from the University of Utah Lowell Bennion Community Service Center, who kept me functioning on an ideal plane. I never lost hope because they insisted on it. Irene Fisher, director at the Bennion Center, taught me that part of my responsibility in having volunteers was to teach the community, to share the lessons I had learned from these children.

My teaching staff for sharing laughter and tears and many long hours. Many of them, like Faye, did the bulk of the work while I received the credit and the attention.

Paul Soria at the shelter, who has always been my friend.

My family, including my parents, in-laws, and grandparents for support and early lessons in love.

Gold Leaf Press for listening and understanding that this work needed to be done. And to Darla Isackson, especially, who arrived in the nick of time to ensure that the book flowed right and, most importantly, felt right.

The community for their support and concern.

And finally, to all the children and their families. I will never learn more anywhere about life and love.

✂

Introduction

When I decided that I wanted to be a teacher, I never dreamed of teaching children in a homeless shelter. But for the past seven years, I have taught at just such a school, the School With No Name, in Salt Lake City, Utah. With widespread poverty changing the face of homelessness in America, more and more of the homeless are families, which means more and more of the homeless are children.

After seven years, I have come to feel strongly that people need to see what I see each day and to know these children. When I speak in behalf of homeless children, the last thing I say to the audience is, "If you could spend just one day at the school, you would be a better person. You would feel so much more in your lives just by experiencing the strength that has come from all of the tragedies these kids have lived through." I wrote this book, finally, to share these things, to introduce you to these children and let you learn from them as I have.

I think if you came to work with me for a day, among other things, you would discover that homelessness is not a "personal" problem. By this I mean that people do not become homeless simply because something is wrong with them. Though there are those among the homeless who choose a transient lifestyle, most guests at the family shelter do not fall into this category. Guests come to the family shelter when their other social networks fail. The complexities surrounding so many of the "causes" of homelessness—substance abuse, mental illness, lack of education, insufficient housing, and domestic violence, as well as poverty—extend beyond the individual. The individual bears the brunt of the burden and, often, the better part of the responsibility, but that does not excuse the rest of us from caring.

Societal apathy, the lack of affection and action in behalf of fellow human beings, or simply not knowing how or when to help has left people falling through the cracks of practically every social institution—family, church, school systems, government agencies. Poverty exacerbates the dysfunctional experiences which leave some people on the streets, but their problems are problems of people, people who have been passed over by a society in which, too often, we have forgotten how to love one another. Because we have forgotten this, we tend to do things backwards and act only when things get tough. We fix rather than prevent. We imprison instead of educating. We use violence in the place of dialogue.

The lessons shared in this book extend far beyond homelessness. They are lessons in how to love, in giving and receiving, in the power love has to heal and to help. They are also lessons in how keeping silent or acting unkindly can affect a human being and how the damage done to one person can sometimes be passed on to the next generation. The children whose stories I share have loved me, taught me new depths of both pain and compassion, and shown me how vital it is for each of us to take care of our own—to love those around us in our families and communities enough to make a small difference in their lives.

I want you to have the chance to feel for the children I have come to know, to cheer for Alex, struggle with Tucker, share peace and security with Maria. I want you to be unable to forget these children. I want you to walk in their shoes a moment and be moved by their experiences in a way that will provoke you to reach out and make a difference in your world. Nobody can tell you what you can do to act, but I hope you will recognize the need and learn that if we spend our time judging, we may lose the opportunity to serve. ✏

Beyond the Blackboard

Lessons on Love from the School With No Name

Toughen Up
and Teach Them

As I traveled up and down side roads in search of the west-side address I had jotted on the back of an envelope, I was alarmed to think that here, in the middle of nowhere, I was getting close to my destination. My search had brought me to a series of run-down backstreets interlaced by railroad tracks that seemed to go on forever. Naked trees and warehouses stood out against the January sky. Frantically I wiped the steam from the car window with my sleeve and struggled to read the street sign crusted with frozen, gray snow. Damn the district anyway for giving me this job.

Turning the corner onto a one-way street, I spotted the shelter and in the distance what looked like the flicker of a campfire in the gutter at the edge of the street, sheltered from view by one of the pillars of the freeway on-ramp. Men and women milled around the streets, some carrying large bags and packs. Some, dressed in bulky layers of second-hand castoffs, still hunched their shoulders against the cold. As I edged forward in my car, I was met by glassy eyes and blank stares, as though the shades were pulled down to guard their privacy.

Children of all ages rushed about outside a metal shed—running as though they were playing some strange game. They reminded me of birds, flailing their arms, never staying put. As I parked beside the shed, a boy with golden hair hanging wildly over his eyes hurtled towards me, then crouched to tie his shoelace in front of my car. He must have sensed I was watching him because suddenly he flipped his hair out of his face and glared at me. His "I'll get you before you get me" look hit me like a hard fist in the stomach as the realization dawned: this kid could be one of my students. When I had dreamed of being a teacher, I had always imagined myself hurrying up the steps of a spacious brick school in a neighborhood with giant oak trees, a church nearby, and children whose eyes were filled with hope and wonder. How on earth had I ended up *here*?

It was my family's fault. After months of listening to my family hand out advice as families do, I had applied with the local school district in 1987, just before Christmas break, hoping that my name would get lost in the shuffle or that the district would recognize that my half-hearted application was not to be taken seriously. It was true that I had gone into education because I loved children and wanted to make a difference—but I wanted to make a difference later. Burned-out after almost six years of college, I longed to stay home for a while with my own children, who were two and six. I was even considering talking my husband, Greg, into having another one. I was only twenty-three, and I figured there was plenty of time for a career. However, within a week of putting in my application I found myself sitting across a wide desk from a businesslike personnel director.

"Mrs. Bess," he informed me, "I've been going over your application. You seem to have all the necessary qualifications for the only mid-year opening we have at the present. It's an afternoon teaching position at the community homeless shelter."

My hands began to tremble. This wasn't what I had expected for a first job—for any job. "I'm not trained in adult education," I admitted.

"This is the family shelter. You'll be teaching kindergarten through sixth grade at the shelter school," the personnel director said matter-of-factly. "Report to the metal shed at the compound under the Sixth South viaduct the day after Christmas vacation."

The brave exterior I had so carefully practiced for my first "real-world" experience started to crack. I couldn't even picture the job he was describing, and my fear of the unknown was almost unbearable. Feisty and stubborn I might be, but I didn't want to teach six grades at a homeless shelter. I didn't want to report to a shed.

"I'm not an experienced teacher. Are you sure I'll be right for this job?" I asked hopefully, seeking some reassurance— or, even better, a way out.

"Of course you will," he replied.

I was not convinced.

If I hadn't been convinced before, I certainly wasn't now as I surveyed the neighborhood. Slowly, I rolled down the car window, trying to find the courage to ask where the shelter school was.

Tap, tap, tap...

My scream caught in my throat as I saw a wild-looking man with disheveled hair standing at the passenger window. I held my breath as he hobbled around my car.

"You lost, ma'am?" the man asked kindly.

Disarmed by his courtesy, I responded, "I think so."

"Where ya trying to get to?" the man asked. Extending a shaky hand, I gave him the address. He smiled, a toothless smile with bits of breakfast clinging in his beard, but he spoke with a warmth I will never forget.

"I'll bet you're the new teacher," he said.

"I am," I responded, wishing I wasn't.

"You got the right place. I'm Joe," he declared while he held open my door for me. Then he proceeded to give me a crash course on street survival: *Don't talk to nobody you don't know. Don't forget to lock your car. Don't look afraid.* I had broken every rule so far, especially the last one. I hurriedly locked my door, and Joe led me past the shelter to meet the handful of people standing around the fire. "We have to build it up close to the viaduct there so the police or the shelter staff won't see it and make us put it out," he explained while I slipped along behind him in my heels.

The small circle around the fire opened to let us in. A heavy woman who sat spread-legged on the curb was cooking over the flames. As Joe and I approached, she called out over her shoulder. A few moments later, some of the children I had seen snuck over and she passed out food to them.

"This here's Gretchen," Joe said, pointing to the bulky woman tending the fire. "About half of them kids back there must be hers." Gretchen smiled and offered me a cup of coffee, which I declined. Joe introduced me as the new teacher, and the others around the fire began shooting questions my way.

"Where ya from?"

"How did you end up with this job?"

"Where did you teach before?"

They laughed when I admitted this was my first real job.

"Well, honey," Gretchen said, "you ain't got nowhere to go but up."

The unexpected rapport warmed the biting cold as we stood there around the fire, sharing shy smiles and real talk. I gathered that the campfire was against shelter rules, and this group tended to keep to themselves, though they assured me they were glad to have another teacher for their children. I began to relax just a little.

A little girl, anxious to meet the new teacher, cautiously approached me.

"You gonna be my teacher?" she asked.

"I sure am," I responded, feeling relieved to see a smiling student. She had beautiful olive skin and wore her hair in a long braid. "What's your name?"

"Robyn."

"Don't you have class in the mornings, Robyn?"

"It's recess," Robyn said as she reached for my hand. "How come you're shaking?"

"I'm a little cold," I told her. It was only half a lie.

With her tiny, cold hand wrapped in mine we left the fire and threaded our way through the children crisscrossing the gravel play area. They screamed and chased each other around like kids do anywhere, while the cloudy sky cast a random pattern of light and shadow on twelve white-and-orange trailers lined up in two rows of six. These made up the living quarters at the shelter. None of them looked big enough to hold more than a couple of beds and a box or two of belongings. Since the only lavatory was located at the front of the lot, the shelter reminded me of a rundown campground with an outhouse.

While gawking around trying to take all this in, I walked right into a gentleman coming out of one of the trailers.

"Excuse me," I stammered as I looked into the dark, calm eyes of a tall Hispanic man in his sixties. I stuck out my hand. "I'm Stacey Bess, the new teacher."

"My name is John," he smiled. "I take care of the office. If you need any help, just come running." I liked his friendly, down-to-earth manner, and I had a long list of questions already, but my new friend Robyn was in a hurry.

"Let's go in the school now, Teacher," she said, tugging me along. She led me through the dayroom housed in a gray, metal shed where the families congregated for warmth. A musty smell filled my nostrils and the sense of angry hopelessness that filled the room started my heart pounding again. Unkempt parents slouched in the sagging couches, staring at a television and grumbling at the restless toddlers who ran about on the muddy gold carpet. When a little boy dropped his bottle, a man snapped, "Sit down," as he grabbed the child by the arm and retrieved the bottle. When my eyes met the eyes of the child's mother, she hung her head.

The room felt as though it could boil over any minute, explode in an eruption of despair or violence, and I knew I was way out of my comfort zone. How was I supposed to teach kids here, amidst all *this*?

"This is our school," Robyn said, opening a door in the back of the room and ushering me into an undersized, makeshift classroom that smelled like a P. E. locker room. The morning teacher got up from behind a splintered desk and smiled as she welcomed me and introduced herself as Janet. I must have looked terrified because she quickly put her arm around me as though to keep me from collapsing with fear.

"It is a little overwhelming at first," she said consolingly, "but it gets better." Just then the tow-headed boy who had stopped to tie his shoelace in front of my car pushed past me into the room. The teacher caught him by the back of his coat and held him in a bear hug around his shoulders. "This is Zach," she said. She mussed his hair and laughed as he slipped out of her hug, made his way noisily to the back of the room, and plopped down next to Robyn.

Scanning the room while I slipped off my coat, I spotted a few children too tall to be in elementary school. "Aren't some of these children a little old to be here?" I whispered to Janet.

She simply said, "If they come, teach them. We get children old enough for junior high or high school, but we never turn them away. So many of them are behind in school, and there's always something they can learn."

I would come to adopt her policy as my own soon enough. When any parent at the shelter showed a desire to educate his or her children regardless of their age, it would be my job to feed that desire. But at that moment, the thought of including older children in lesson plans already splitting the seams to accommodate all seven elementary-age grades made this crazy situation all the more overwhelming. I worried about their size, too. The little ones I figured I could handle and win over. The big ones, I wasn't so sure.

"One more question," I said as Janet slipped on her coat. She turned to me with a smile that I knew somehow was the most honest smile I had ever seen. She was happy to be here.

"Why do they call this the School With No Name?" The personnel director had called the school by this name when I had left his office.

"Because it doesn't have a name," she responded simply. "This is temporary, emergency education. A lot of people in the district don't even know we're out here; we don't have a permanent building. Nobody thought of names. The School With No Name is just something the press picked up. It's kind of catchy."

At 12:30, with the door closed, I faced my class. The room was full of coughs and sniffs, and from outside the door came the harsh noises of the dayroom. Zach sat in the back, his white hair sticking out like stray weeds, chewing at a grimy thumbnail. Robyn sat next to him. I now noticed that she wasn't wearing a coat, only a heavy sweater rolled up at the sleeves, and she had fraying, pink leg warmers pulled up over her jeans. There was a little boy with a grubby face wearing a woman's coat that fit him like a tent who was paying absolutely no attention to what was going on at the front of the classroom, and twenty others who looked ragged, unkempt, and tired like the parents I had seen. But in the silly grin from a chubby, Hispanic boy who sat cross-legged on the floor staring up at me, I saw pure child, and my resistance to this place began to waver.

I can do this, I reassured myself as I cleared my throat and looked into the expectant eyes of a roomful of children. I was new, and they had to be curious to know whether I was any match for them. It would turn out to be the one and only time they ever sat quietly and waited for me to speak. Taking advantage of this awesome silence I introduced myself.

"I'm Stacey," I began. "I brought along a little something to help you get to know me." I held up a scrapbook with "ME" pasted on the front cover.

"This is my family," I explained as I opened the book to a picture of the four of us. "This is Greg, my cute husband.

This is our daughter, Nichole, and this is our little boy, Brandon."

So far, so good. Now I wanted to establish some common ground.

"My story starts with my three favorite likes, the three Cs: children, chocolate, and Coke—Diet Coke." As I stood there trying to convince them somehow that I could be one of them, that I could belong in their world, suddenly a mouse raced right across my feet. I jumped to the ceiling, screamed, and would have impressed Michael Jackson with my dance moves. My heart thumped in my throat as I gasped for breath and met the unblinking eyes of thirty kids staring at me in total disgust.

✄

I survived the day, and when the last babbling child reached up for a hug then scooted out the door, I locked myself in the classroom, collapsed across the splintered desk, and sobbed. What the hell am I doing here? I asked myself. It wasn't the mouse that was bothering me, and I knew I was already falling for these kids. But I was overwhelmed, exhausted from the stress of just one day, sickened by the filth, and frightened by what was ahead. I dreaded coming back the next day, and I found myself counting the months until my contract was up in June. There was no way I could make it in the midst of all this deprivation. How could I tell these kids who had nothing that they should care about learning to add and subtract, to spell and read? I told myself I cared too much. It hurt too badly to be here. I couldn't desensitize myself enough to function in this environment.

One thing I was certain about: once I had made it through these few months, I'd quit. I had gone into teaching for the highest of purposes: I wanted to change the world. I believed kids needed to be told they were valuable and talented. I believed they needed to have opinions and power. And I believed I could help. Sure, I could be a little cocky, and I'd always thought I was strong—but I certainly wasn't strong enough for *this*.

In the midst of my despair, I heard a loud knock. Wiping my eyes, I opened the door. John, the staff member I'd met earlier, caught me brushing away the last of my tears.

"The first day's always a hard one," he said.

No kidding.

Shaking his head kindly, he put his arm around me. Then, with the wisdom of a father he spoke some words I still repeat to myself:

"Look, Stacey, we need you here, and you won't be any good to these kids if you go around crying. So toughen up and teach them."

I nodded and promised him I would, though at that moment you could never have convinced me that soon— very soon—I would judge this work worthy of my best efforts and most passionate devotion. ✏

<u>December 1</u>

Dear Diary: My teacher just finished reading a very funny book to us.
It's called *The Best Christmas Pageant Ever.* I liked it because I understand about kids who don't have nothin'. The part I liked best about
the book was that someone as important as Jesus didn't have a home
to live in, either.

P.S. The boys' and girls' activities tonight are at the YMCA. Don't
think I'll go. The coach calls us the homeless kids group in front of the
other kids. Jamie's family had to move out last week, so I don't have
anybody to go with, anyway.

What Happens to the Promise?

The children at the School With No Name accepted me at once, insisting on hugs and bringing me curious gifts. Rachel slipped a hot cereal packet into my pocket. Kevin brought me a broken string of plastic beads. Mitchell handed me a tattered, cardboard clown and told me it would help me feel happy. They were hungry to learn, almost desperate for the safe, kid-type activities and atmosphere of the classroom. I wanted to make a difference, and if there were anyplace where a difference needed to be made, I figured, it was here.

Usually it was what was happening outside the doors that made me wonder—listening to the babies cry, the dads yell at the moms, the moms scream at the babies. It was the cars that circled the shelter at night so the families who slept in them could use the shelter facilities in the morning. It was the quiet desperation of families in poverty.

I felt surrounded by loss. Nobody had anything. I had never thought about needing to find gas money to get to the store to buy food with food stamps. Suddenly I found myself considering whether I took almost everything in my life for granted. I saw depression, especially in the parents, who often seemed lethargic and gloomy. Passing through the day-room and looking into the faces was like watching a movie in slow motion and black-and-white, no color, no light, just mundane living filled with hopelessness. By my standards a lot of the children looked unkempt, and I translated this to mean uncared for. Their hair looked as if it hadn't been brushed in months; they ate things after dropping them on the ground. I was appalled, too, that the families at the shelter accepted the conditions. I saw them as people, yet they weren't living like people. I had a hard time believing that this could be home to them.

What I had to learn was that this was all these people had right then.

For the first month I came home worn out, in tears, and with headaches the size of the Wasatch Mountains that surround the city. *I've never been a quitter,* I would tell myself at nights, and once I begin something I am determined to do it right and look good. Still, I was light-years away from feeling really comfortable. Just as I'd begin to think I was standing firm, the ground would crumble underneath me and leave me shaken again—like the day two of my young students came to school dressed in suits, accompanied by a stranger.

"We came to say good-bye," they said bravely.

"Where are you going?" I asked.

"I don't know," the older one explained, "just away from Mom and Rick. They don't want us anymore."

My mouth gaped open, and I struggled for words. What was I supposed to say? I gathered the boys up in big hugs and told them I would miss them and that I was sure they would like it where they were going. But I was just as confused as they were. When I cornered another woman at the shelter who knew the boys' mother, she explained to me in private that the mother had been given an ultimatum by her new husband: Get rid of the kids or I'm out of here. She had chosen the husband over the children and given them up for adoption.

"How could she?" I blurted out.

The rest of the day was a blur. I stumbled through my lessons and administrative duties zombielike, until I got to my mother's house to pick up my own children. As soon as she said, "How was your day," the tears poured out along with the story of the two boys given away by their mother. "How about a little rocking?" Mom quietly asked while I sobbed uncontrollably in the middle of her living room. I nodded, and she took me by the hand and led me to the rocking chair where we cuddled up together and she tenderly rocked me as though I were a baby.

Quietly she held me while I cried myself out. "That place is killing me," I sobbed.

"No one could see what you've seen and not feel bad."

"It just isn't fair. It isn't right."

"I know," she said, stroking my back. "You've always wanted things to be fair, even when you were a little girl, and they just aren't."

This wasn't the first afternoon in my adult life that I had been rocked in the rocking chair. This was a family tradition as natural as Sunday dinner or hugs at bedtime. As far back as I can remember, whenever I was in a crisis—even during my crazy, rebellious teen years—it was always OK to collapse and cry with Mom in the rocker. I had learned to love and to pray in that rocking chair with my mother, and now in my time of need, it became my place of healing.

I did a lot of rocking with Mom after school those first months, and I said a lot of angry prayers when I got home. "God, how can you let children suffer so much?" my mind would shout. "Why have you put me in this place where it seems there is so little I can do to help?" Then, after the anger left, my prayer would change, "I can't do this alone, God," I insisted, "I need your help!" With the prayers, the rocking, the crying, the questioning, I survived emotionally and got rid of enough tension, anger, frustration, and sadness to begin all over again the next day.

✂

As often as not, the next day would begin with Danny teasing me from the doorway of the classroom. "To go to school or to not go to school, that is the question," he'd quote, as he dropped off a younger brother or sister. Then he would follow up with, "What can you teach me today, Teach?"

"I don't know Danny," I would respond, sounding just as sassy as he did. "Come sit down and let's see if I know anything you don't know."

Even though by law the kids in the shelter should have been in school, at that time there was no one around to enforce the rule. Danny came more often than most kids his age. He treated me with an "I like you, but I don't need you" attitude, peeking in the door to make fun of what I was teaching or to shake his finger and say to the kids, "Listen to your teacher." He wanted to listen himself, but it was nothing he was going to let on to. To compromise, he would hang out in the doorway after dropping off a brother or sister. Then, when the lesson started and the focus was elsewhere, he would slowly ease himself into my classroom to sit a while.

Danny was a cowboy-looking kid, a well-built sixteen-year-old with a missing eyetooth and sandy brown hair that I never saw combed. He was a mix, in physique and temperament, of both his parents. His father was a tall, weathered man with a long beard that gave him the look of an ancient rabbi. He walked around mad at the world, cursing everybody. In contrast, his mother was only five feet tall, and when she spoke I had to listen very carefully to understand her, since she had lost all but her front two bottom teeth. With her long, gray hair, she reminded me of the witch in Hansel and Gretel, but her gentle manner made her more like a Mother Goose.

Danny was this big, gentle human being who had picked up an "I-don't-give-a-damn" attitude from his father, but had inherited his mother's tenderness as well. I often saw him holding and soothing one of the children, a big brother at large to the entire shelter population. We took an immediate liking to each other. At least I liked him.

My first real sign that Danny was warming up to me came one morning when I arrived at the school and found that someone had broken into my classroom. I was furious. We had so little to begin with. Now somebody had stolen an old TV and VCR we used to watch videos sometimes as a reward for a good week. I was getting ready to go tell John, my friend on the staff, about it and demand that somebody search the trailers, when Danny went against his street conscience and told me who did it, although he let me know there was nothing I could do about it.

"The people who took the stuff didn't know you or they wouldn't have done it," he said. It was a couple staying at the shelter, but their children were preschoolers, and they had no contact with me or the school. They had taken the old television from the classroom and carried it out the back door with a white sheet around it. After assuring me that I would never recover it, Danny gave me a short lesson on how very easy it is to steal and trade the merchandise for drugs or get it to a pawn shop before the police can track it down.

"That's the way things go down here," he said.

"It's not the way you go, though, is it?" I said, calmed down after his explanation.

"I don't need to steal nothing," he told me, though I think he might have had two pairs of pants to his name, and I hadn't seen him in a coat the whole winter. Stealing might have crossed my mind if I had been in his shoes.

"You could *steal* into my classroom a little more," I teased him.

"You can't earn while you learn," he quipped. I knew Danny did odd jobs to help out with the family's expenses, and I had a hard time coming up with arguments against it. I believed kids needed to be in school. I believed the hope for their futures was waiting there. But I understood that when it came down to practical choices between going to school or helping feed the family, any future seemed a long way off.

As we became better friends, Danny did sit in on my class more and more. I was glad to have him because I figured I could count on him if the class ever broke out in a riot.

In the classroom, we always seemed to be operating on the edge of disruption and outburst. The kids moved around and talked out of turn more than I had ever seen in public school. With kids coming and going, parents looking in, me reminding somebody to sit down, be quiet, or what the assignment was they should be working on, the day seemed made up of interruptions. In between the parts of speech or multiplication, we could have anything from a tantrum complete with flying chairs to a contest to see who could belch the entire alphabet. I decided later that the children's emotions are running so high that every minute of their lives is a balancing act just to keep coping. They all have some sort of crisis going on, and relaxing the atmosphere in the classroom helped relax them. I found out soon enough, on a day Danny wasn't there, that I was on the emotional tightrope, too.

Stewart came in late that day, whistling and high-fiving all his sixth-grade buddies while I was trying to explain a writing project. I waited at the chalkboard while he made a big deal out of sitting down. Then came the pencil tapping on the table until I asked him to quit, and he looked up with wide-eyed innocence and asked, "Who, me?" Then the Walkman headphones slid out of his pocket, to be shared with his neighbor. After he got off a couple of dirty jokes then grabbed another student's paper to write something obscene across the top while wandering around the room, I exploded.

"Look," I yelled, with my finger in his face, "I don't get paid enough to put up with your shit. Now sit your butt down in that chair and shut up!" I held his gaze while he lowered himself into his seat. The class became remarkably quiet and polite, while I fumed. But by the time I cooled down, I was embarrassed.

I agonized over the incident all afternoon. I just wanted to hurry the kids out of the classroom so I could rush out and apologize to Stewart's father. I found him after a quick search, told him exactly what I had said, told him I was embarrassed about it, and apologized. He just about doubled over laughing as I finished.

"You just keep it up, Stacey," he said, trying to get his wind back. "That kid had it coming to him."

Danny laughed, too, when he heard about it.

"See what you miss when you don't come to class," I told him, still feeling kind of sheepish.

"What are you worried about it for?" he said.

"I'm a teacher. I'm supposed to be professional. That means you don't yell and swear at your students."

Danny shrugged. He was toying with an art print I had brought to class that day. I love the fine arts—painting, music, dance—and I brought prints to discuss in class, trying to help the children develop both appreciation and critical thinking skills. I learned that I could corner Danny before class, brief him about the artist and the painting, and he could stand up and teach the lesson almost as well as I could. I always included something bizarre or unique about the artist—that Van Gogh cut off his own ear or Degas painted all his ballerinas to look sad. Little did Danny realize how much he was learning.

"Why don't you just give in and accept that learning feels good?" I joked with him that afternoon.

"What's so important about learning this stuff?" he said, handing me the picture.

"It doesn't have to be important. You can just like it. It can just be interesting."

"My mom and dad don't care. If they didn't need to graduate or anything, neither do I," he shrugged. It was a response I would come to hear from some of my students far too often.

"It's a changing world. You're going to need an education to get a good job," I reasoned.

"I'll probably just join the Army or something. No, the

Marines," he changed his mind. "You don't have to know nothing to do that."

"You do if you want to be a general," I offered.

I was learning quickly that many parents who are chronically or semi-transient don't put much emphasis on their children's education. When someone ends up on the street after years of public schooling, the response is often, "So what good did all that school do me anyway?" Often, too, the family needs the older kids to work. Education doesn't help the family financially in the short term. I needed them to see the value of education as a long-term investment. Danny should have been a junior in high school, but he had been in and out of schools so much while his family drifted from place to place that he was about two grade levels behind.

In Danny's case, I was the only person encouraging him to get an education. Desperately, I searched for subjects that would intrigue him, while struggling to get him to enroll in school.

"Why don't you just give it a try?" I asked him.

"The only thing I liked about school is wrestling. I'm damned good, you know," he looked at me challengingly. I couldn't argue with that. The kid was built like a Mack truck. Then I realized that this was my in. He'd wrestled before in another school and kept longing for it. I told Danny I would check to see if the local high school had a wrestling team.

"Will you register and try out if they do?" I said.

I didn't know that the wrestling season was almost over, and apparently neither did Danny, because to my surprise, he consented.

Friday morning I arrived at the shelter at 6:45 a.m. to take Danny to the local high school. In the dark, I climbed the two steps up to the family's trailer, hanging onto the doorknob to keep from slipping on the icy metal, and knocked quietly. In a few moments, Danny appeared at the door sleepy-eyed and apologizing for not being ready.

"I have to take my little brothers and sisters with us. My parents didn't come home last night, and I don't want the shelter to call the police," Danny said. I knew by now, as he did, that parents risked charges of abandonment if they didn't come home at night and the staff didn't know where they were. Inside, the trailer reminded me of an old camper. It had two beds, with little space in between, and a nightstand. The wood panelling was a depressing, dark brown. Danny's brothers and sisters slept packed in wall to wall, and their little bodies bumped and tangled as I helped Danny get them out of bed and dressed.

Finally, the eight of us headed off in my little green Celica. While we waited at a red light, Danny leaned over from the backseat and turned up the radio loud enough for everyone within a block to hear. I reached to turn it down, then told myself it was only a few blocks to the school. Two blocks later, as I was watching the kids in the rearview mirror, bouncing to the music and laughing, I noticed a police officer slowly approaching the side of the car. I quickly snapped the radio off and told the kids to sit quietly so I wouldn't get a ticket.

Suddenly, the kids began frantically rolling down the windows. Danny leaned over the front seat and yelled, "Hey Teach, did you fart?"

I was humiliated. "No, I didn't," I responded, trying to act the part of the indignant school teacher and wondering why I wasn't teaching sweet little second-graders who would call me "Mrs. Bess" instead of "Teach."

Danny laughed. "Well, it must have been me." The kids joined in his laughter as they leaned over the seats to stick their heads out the windows of my two-door car for fresh air.

The police officer had pulled up and was now rolling his window down to chastise me.

"Please get the children into the car," he said with authority. I began to apologize, but Danny broke in before I could pull my thoughts together and get a word out.

"But sir," he said dramatically, "I farted and we'll all die of suffocation if we get back in." At that moment death didn't sound too bad. The officer couldn't help but smile. The look on my face is something I'm sure he will never forget. I was embarrassed; I was frightened; I had all these kids with no seat belts on hanging out the windows, and Danny had caught me completely off guard when I was trying to act the part of the proper school marm. The officer started to laugh and waved me on my way.

We finally made it to the high school with a lot of whining and griping, but no more serious encounters. The children were hungry and tired, and they wanted to know where their mom and dad were. After seating all six of them on the couch in the office, Danny and I approached the secretary. I could see that she was swamped by what looked to be a classful of students milling around in the office. Slowly and quietly, I introduced Danny. He was living at a homeless shelter, I explained, and this high school would be the easiest for him to attend.

After a look at Danny and me, the secretary yelled across the room to one of the administrators, "Hey, Allen, what do I do with this homeless kid?" I stood in absolute shock, while the other students in the office craned their necks to look. Stung by her insensitivity, I glanced at Danny and prayed silently, *Please don't cry.* But I could see he didn't feel what I felt. Suddenly it made me even more angry that this young man had been treated so callously that this sort of unkindness did not strike him as unacceptable.

I didn't understand then that secretaries have an extra paperwork load with transient children, paperwork that is often painstakingly filled out only to have these students move on within a few days or weeks. I did know that we were adding to this secretary's stress that morning. But to say what she did in front of Danny's peers was unthinkable. I found myself feeling very possessive of Danny, and I didn't know if I wanted to turn him over to this school or not. I bit my tongue for his sake, to keep from causing a bigger scene.

We made it through the registration process and Danny proved to be a much bigger person than I will probably ever be. When we got out to the car, all he said was, "That's why we have the shelter school."

Danny began school the following Monday. We eventually got all his fees waived so that he could enjoy a cost-free and carefree opportunity to learn. The wrestling coach agreed to let him come to workouts with the team, even though the season was almost over. Things were finally looking up. Danny had found a reason to go to school. I had big plans for him: finish the year, then summer school to get him caught up. He'd graduate, and I'd help find him a scholarship to go to college. But, as the saying goes, all good things must come to an end.

One morning when I knocked on the door to pick Danny up for school, there was no answer, only a dreadful silence.

"They're gone. They got mad and left last night," the monitor said.

"Gone where?" I demanded.

"Who knows? You all right Ms. Bess?"

In a daze I walked back to the car. I sat there for an hour, staring at the ugly, rust-spotted trailers, at the cars full of more people parked in a half-circle around the shelter, at my new world that hadn't been so bleak with Danny in it. It just wasn't fair, I told God angrily. I didn't get enough time with him. As I leaned my head back against the car seat, I asked myself over and over, "Why?" Why, when I had finally reached this kid? Why, when he was doing so well?

I found out later that Danny had suffered the results of his parents' decisions. John told me that during their ninety-day stay, his parents had made no attempt toward the self-sufficiency goals required by the shelter. If they hadn't left when they did, they probably would have been asked to leave the next week.

After a few weeks, Danny did get in touch with me, but he wasn't in school. He said maybe the next fall he would try it again, and I should watch for his name in the papers when the state wrestling championships came around. Danny kept in touch for a time, but for a little while I found it hard to feel hope for any of these children. I convinced myself that every ninety days when one left, I would lose another one, and I went home after work and cried.

✄

I remembered Danny's story the following year, when opportunities to speak in behalf of the children began to come. I started accepting speaking engagements in desperation. I wanted people to understand these kids, and I wanted help. It also proved therapeutic—I could share my heartbreak as I talked about what I was trying to deal with and tried to let people know what they could do. Over time I spoke to church groups, conferences on homelessness and for those who serve troubled youth, Kiwanis and Rotary clubs, and lots of large businesses who wanted to put something back into their community.

As I went along, I learned what inspired people. You couldn't just tell people to help; you had to make them fall in love with the children. I would begin by telling them stories about kids I was working with at the time or kids who had impacted my life. At the end of each story, I would explain what I had learned from this particular child. Regardless of the audience, I always asked one hard, soul-searching question: Where were you and where was I when this father or mother or child could have used a friend? Somebody once said to me that when you are telling the truth, it is an easy thing to do, and spirits talk to one another. I found that when I stood up and told something that desperately needed to be told, it hit the right spot and people listened.

Danny's story was one I had in mind at a professional conference to discuss the education of homeless children.

There, as politely as I could, I blasted the system. I was appalled that as intelligent, educated administrators and teachers we could not make the system work as it was meant to for all children. We had laws set up to provide equal educational opportunities, laws to guarantee that no matter where you were, you had a right to be educated. But too often, the laws didn't seem to be working.

I was appalled at the lack of understanding shown for underprivileged students when we didn't follow guidelines we had established, such as one stating that impoverished families should not be required to pay fees. I was appalled that children on the free school lunch program were not being fed because their number had been entered wrong on a computer. The school lunch might be the only meal they would get, but the bureaucratic rules stood in the way, and for seventy cents we couldn't feed a child.

My point at that meeting, and others I would speak at later, was that it makes no sense to turn away a family because they don't have school records or a permanent address. The primary goal of education should be to get the child into the classroom; you can deal with records later. For so many, getting their kids to school once represents a milestone that says they now value education. They may have traveled a hard road to get there. They may have used their last gas money. So you don't turn them away. You give them a positive experience. You give the kids a little extra help, a little boost; you keep an eye on them so they can succeed.

Almost everybody was sympathetic, once the word got out.

✂

These were all things I was only beginning to become aware of when Danny left. After only five months, I had plenty of hard lessons left to learn. One of the hardest would be that one person can't be everywhere to motivate and to love every child. I would learn it quickly, as I did with Danny, and I would be reminded of it over and over again. These children must connect with other teachers and adults who will hang on to them and keep them from falling through the cracks. Almost anyone who has faith in the power we have to change the lives of others can make the difference. All it takes is getting involved and believing that you can make a child's life better—and having the knowledge and heart to go to bat against the system. It helps if you can cry a little, too, because you don't win them all.

At the school, my vow to walk away from the shelter program in June was starting to sound hollow and empty. Somewhere along the way in those first five months, I had come to feel at home in that battered little classroom, and a little voice was beginning to nudge me with the powerful words, "You can make such a difference if you'll just stay." I didn't know yet the best way to make that difference, but I knew that in trying to find hope and a chance for kids like Danny, I had found a cause. ✏

The Giving Is Enough

The love notes the children made for me to say good-bye as we closed up the school that first June cinched it. I promised I'd be back, even though most of them would have moved on. But some of them would be back, some as students again, some just to "call home" at the one safe place they had known. It was something that would keep me coming back year after year—the fear that one of the children would come looking for me, and I wouldn't be there.

I had butterflies as I drove back to the shelter in August. I would be on my own this year—Janet, the morning teacher, wouldn't be back—but I had tried to turn my fear into new energy and lesson plans based on the latest academic theories. Still, the classroom almost dampened my spirits. I came a few days early to clean, but after I scrubbed with Lysol, stacked and restacked, the only thing I'd improved was the smell. College had prepared me to teach in a schoolroom with a blackboard, neat rows of desks, and an American flag in the front of the room. Sure, I'd been warned we could be short some books, or the class might be a little overcrowded. But this? I gazed around the room in total frustration. Not one thing in the room was fit for a child. The desks were chipped and rammed together, all the books were heavily used and battered, and the room was poorly lit and cramped—each time the class needed to retrieve a book from the cinder block shelves, the entire back row had to stand up and move their desks. What these kids called their school was nothing more than a heap of makeshift hand-me-downs, all packed inside an old metal shed in the middle of nowhere.

The Pledge of Allegiance hung on the board behind the teacher's desk. "And justice for all," it read. My eyes locked on that phrase, and suddenly it was full of new meaning and irony.

"Bull," I said out loud, and I took a little anger and indignation with me into that year as well, figuring it just might come in handy.

✁

I started out that second year with some things to prove. I was in charge now, and I decided that meant that school was going to be important and the kids were going to be there. To accomplish this, I began an aggressive campaign of knocking on doors when it got close to nine o'clock and my classroom was still almost empty, something I had done a little of the year before if I happened to be there in the morning. Already I found I had a strange confidence among these people. Nobody was going to hurt me here, so up and down I went, between the trailers and around the parked cars, pounding on doors and yelling, "School starts at nine, be there."

The kids would come hustling over the gravel lot, with their hair sticking up all over and a bowl of cereal in their hands. Most mornings we went through our first lesson with the accompaniment of crunching and slurps as the children finished their breakfast, but I didn't mind. I was just glad they were there.

As school got under way that year, I also noticed that the shelter had a new monitor. The administrators sometimes hired residents as monitors to help maintain and run the shelter. I ran into the new one on my way back to the classroom after one of my morning student roundups. He was carrying breakfast cereal to the dayroom.

"Let me get the door," I said, because he had his hands full.

"Thanks," the monitor mumbled, but didn't make eye contact. I stared, startled by a soft, feminine voice.

"Hey," I said.

When the monitor turned to glance up at me, I saw that she was a woman, a striking young woman, over six feet tall with high cheekbones and enormous, sparkling blue eyes. She wore no makeup and had her black hair buzzed in a short, spiky cut. A huge pair of Levi's and a leather jacket camouflaged her figure from top to toe, and she moved with the sure, determined motions of a powerful man.

"I'm Stacey," I ventured. "I teach at the school."

The monitor nodded.

"And you are . . .?" I encouraged.

"Karen," she answered and went on her way.

"How long has Karen been here?" I asked John later in the day, while we sat at a couple of students' desks in the stuffy schoolroom, getting reacquainted after the summer.

"A couple of weeks."

"I thought she was a man the first time I saw her."

"That's the way she wants it," John said.

"Why?" I asked.

"She just wants to be tough," John said as he got up to leave. "Welcome back."

"You thought I wasn't coming back, didn't you?" I teased.

"I knew it all the time," John smiled.

✂

Most of Karen's work brought her to the dayroom, which was adjacent to the school, and where we couldn't help running into each other. With the staff and adult guests around the shelter, she was tough, foul-mouthed, and independent, never letting down that exterior toughness. My efforts to be friendly to Karen as the days went by were largely rebuffed. She made it very clear that she viewed me as an outsider, a proper and prudish snob who had no clue about how life had been for someone like her.

With the children in the dayroom, though, it was different. She wasn't very talkative, but she would stop to listen to them, join in some game for a minute, or pick up a toddler.

I guessed that she knew the pain and fear of having nowhere to go, no safe place or security, no possessions, and she had empathy for these children who were suffering the same pain. I guessed, too, that her callousness was a front, and I got angry about Karen's protective walls being put up to ward off the rest of us. How could a human being I was sure was so hungry to be loved be such a porcupine?

Something kept me coming back to Karen, drew me to her, even if it was just the challenge. She was determined to prove that I had no place in and couldn't understand her world, and to do that she would make herself as unlovable as possible. I was just as determined to show her that I could really belong—and that I could love her in spite of herself.

So every time I passed her in the dayroom I would say something to try to strike up a conversation. More often than not, she would come back with something cynical or biting— usually something to try to shock me or convince me what a bad person she was. One day when she had on some especially baggy pants, I asked her where she got them.

"I stole them," she replied defiantly. "You got a problem with that?"

"Yeah," I said, "they don't fit."

"You think I should dress like you? All sleek and proper in little sweaters and skirts? Nobody on the streets going to relate to that."

This was her favorite accusation—that I was a "proper" lady. I didn't think I was so prissy. I carried a leather briefcase and tried to dress and act professionally, but Karen didn't see the silliness that went on in the classroom, where we dipped our feet in pudding to make animal tracks and the kids tried to shock me by writing naughty poetry. On the other hand, Karen let me know that she wasn't proper in any way. She didn't hide her serious drug and alcohol problems and bragged about the tough life she had had in and out of trouble and foster care.

"You don't fool me with your attitude," I challenged while we watched the kids playing in the gravel yard at recess. "You love people a lot more than you let on."

Karen peered at me from underneath her baseball cap.

"What do you want to know me for?" she said over the shrieks from the kids at play.

"You're interesting to me, and I want to be your friend."

"Why?" she demanded.

"I don't know," I said honestly. "There's just something about you that I like." And it was true. It didn't make much sense to me either, unless I just admired her basic rebellious attitude, but it was true.

For about three weeks she constantly challenged me, refusing to admit that we might have anything in common and insisting I was too proper, too uptown for my work. Then, out of the blue, she invited me to go out one night with her and another one of the resident mothers.

"Me and Mel are going out Friday, we want you to come," she said.

"Going where?" I asked.

"Just out," she said. "Just to have some fun. Be a little different from your kind of fun."

"Sure," I said. "What time?" I had no idea what I was really getting into, but I wasn't willing to back down from the challenge.

All week long, Karen and Mel taunted me and made me promise over and over again that I wouldn't back out.

"Will I be safe?" I asked, and they giggled.

"Sure. What do you think, we run with a bunch of animals?" Mel said. "We won't let anything happen to you. Hell, I need someone to teach my kid how to read come Monday morning."

Friday came, and I was nervous. Feeling a little anxious and curious, I grinned at the sight of my two special friends who were dressed the part for a night out on the town. Mel wore a slinky black top, tight jeans, and heels. Karen sported her leather jacket. Suddenly, in jeans and a t-shirt, I was the one who was underdressed.

"I hope you're not as boring as you dress," Mel teased, as we headed downtown. "We're gonna teach you how to have fun; you take life too serious," Mel went on as she guided me through the unfamiliar west-side streets to get to the pool hall both of them kept raving about. Whenever I asked, "Where are we?" both simply told me not to worry, they wouldn't let anything happen to me, and then giggled. As I turned to the right for the last time, both Mel and Karen shouted, "There it is!" I said a quiet prayer and hit the power locks on the doors just as Karen grabbed for the handle.

"You gonna let us out of this car?" she said.

"Sorry, just a habit," I responded, feeling like a fool, struggling to find the button. Sensing my nervousness, they began to reassure me that their peers would adore me. Mel promised to introduce me to everyone.

"They've heard all about you already. We talk about you all the time." As we approached the front door, I noticed a lot of eyes on me. I was way out of my element, but I was beginning to consider myself no stranger to unfamiliar circumstances. "God, help me," I said inside and walked cautiously toward my first new acquaintance.

What happened at the bar was that we had a good time. We shot some pool, and I nursed a Coke while Karen and Mel partied it up. Karen relaxed, we talked, and I enjoyed their company so much that I didn't realize how late it was.

"Guys, I gotta go. My family's going to be worrying," I said finally, feeling a little frantic about the time I had let go by without even noticing.

"You were having fun." Mel sighed as she placed her arms around me. Karen stood behind her, watching me with a little smile on her face. Mel was right, I had had fun. These were real people, and I left that night reminded that it doesn't matter where you live or how much money you make, everyone wants to be loved, listened to, and heard. My first years on the job required abandoning a lot of stereotypes that just didn't pan out when you got to know real people.

✂

Karen must have decided something, too, that night.

"You're an okay lady," she said as she peeked her head into my classroom early on the following Monday morning. Karen and Mel had experienced the same feelings for me as I had for their peers. They dressed differently than I did; they partied differently than I did; but that didn't mean we couldn't have anything in common.

A few weeks later Mel moved out of the shelter. I was accepting good-byes as a constant part of my job, though they weren't getting any easier, even knowing that almost anything was better than the environment of a shelter. Karen took Mel's leaving hard. She connected with very few people, and it always seemed that she chose those who would be leaving soon. Karen and I grew closer in an attempt to fill the loss that she was feeling after Mel's move.

As Karen began to open herself up to me, I found out that she was extremely artistic, yet she didn't allow herself to feel her worth through her talents. In the afternoons after Mel left, I would talk Karen into showing me her sketchbook so I could thumb through her work to praise her. Through the many hours we spent together, I got my first real lesson in the effects of an unstable childhood. Her mother was an unmarried, illiterate teenager when both Karen and her sister were born. She couldn't cope with her own life, much less nurture two little girls, so at a young age, Karen was placed in foster care, then into an orphanage, then back into foster care. Karen's mother would never give permission for Karen to be adopted, so Karen never had stability. Karen and her sister would be placed in a home, then their mother would come and steal them away and keep them until she was tired of them.

Karen had no luck with foster families until she was sixteen, when she moved to Utah and lived with the only family that did not physically or sexually abuse her. "I remember one Christmas when I was a little girl being locked up in the closet because I wasn't good enough to be part of the family," Karen said one day, showing little emotion. "All I ever remember about being a kid was feeling either scared or lonely or mad." This, I figured, was where her mode of dress had come from. She would say it was just her style, just "me," but what it really said was, "I'm not a little girl anymore. I'm someone you can't hurt like that."

Her stories kept me up at night while my mind raced, wondering where all the good people had been in Karen's life. The safe foster homes. The friends. She would tell me, "You don't know what it's like to suffer. You grew up in a home with a mother and a father. You never wanted for anything." Then I would share some of the memories from my own childhood with her, trying to prove I could empathize. My parents had divorced. I'd been the wounded peacemaker, soaking up hurt while I watched the fighting and discord in my family as my stepfather and the rest of us adjusted to our new roles. I'd had to grow up fast, married and pregnant at sixteen. Even in "regular" families people struggle and aren't perfect. I had my own scars and understood better than she realized.

But the biggest tragedy of Karen's background was that it had left her no sense of her worth as a person and as a woman. Since she felt she had no value, there seemed to be nothing to lose by destroying herself with drugs and alcohol. She could see no possibilities in the future for a happiness that had always eluded her in the past and no way out of her downward spiral. She had no motivation for giving up her habits, and it was one thing she didn't want to talk about.

There was something else, too. Karen hadn't told me everything yet.

✁

One cold October morning, hustling in to find refuge from the cold wind in the office trailer, I happened upon the most beautiful newborn baby I had ever seen.

"Whose baby is this?" I inquired as I couldn't see any one around it could belong to, and the baby lay half naked on the cold floor.

John spoke to me as if I were functioning on another planet. "Silly, that's Karen's baby." It took me a minute to find my voice.

"Karen, the new monitor?" I said finally, feeling very puzzled. "She never said anything to me about having a baby. Why wouldn't she have told me she had a child? It isn't very old," I thought out loud, searching my brain for a timeline that would work. I must have looked very troubled because John explained that Karen had been a resident at the women's shelter until the baby was born, and then she came here.

"She started with us about six weeks ago, just before school started," he said. That was about when I had met her.

Karen came in a few minutes later. "Who wants to take my baby home tonight while I work?" she said, not knowing that I was sitting behind the front desk looking through the daily log. When I sat up at the sound of her voice, she looked at me in horror.

Before either of us could speak, another monitor offered to take the baby while Karen worked her shift later.

A few hours passed before Karen peeked into my classroom, where I was timing some of my students on a math test. She had to wait to speak until one of the endless trains that rumbled by only a few yards away had passed. The trains shook the classroom during the day and kept some of the children awake at nights.

"Are you angry at me?" Karen said after the noise died down, with genuine fear in her voice.

"Of course not. I'm a little surprised that you didn't tell

me you had a little girl, but I guess that you were coming to that in time." Karen shrugged.

"I'll bet you're a fine mother," I continued. Her head hung and I knew that things were not going well in the mother-hood department.

The following morning I couldn't shake the thought of Karen and her baby, another child born to a mother who felt little self-worth and who would be mostly incapable of providing security to her child. I was looking out the filthy windows when I spied the silhouette of a large figure in bulky clothes walking briskly under the Sixth South viaduct. It was a woman carrying a bundle against her body as if she were trying to keep them both safe from the cold or something that was following them. I knew it was Karen. School wasn't scheduled to begin for ten minutes—just enough time for me to run and meet her halfway down the street and offer some help and a little understanding.

Karen was shaking when I came up next to her. She looked at me with red, swollen eyes that begged me to stop the world and let her off.

"What can I do?" I asked, hoping that she would let me take the baby into my arms. And then she began to cry.

"Please take her," Karen pleaded, holding out her little daughter. "I'm so mad at her right now. She's screamed all night and I couldn't get her to stop." Later I would learn that the baby wasn't getting the proper nutrition and was slowly starving. Not sure right then whether to hold Karen or the baby, I carefully balanced the little bundle in my left arm and wrapped my right around Karen.

"What's her name?" I asked.

"Liza."

"Why don't you let me take Liza to class with me while you get a cup of coffee and unwind. We'll be fine and you need a few minutes alone." After a little coaxing Karen let me take the baby with me. With Karen's daughter cradled in one arm,

I wrote the day's requirements on the board, while the children chattered behind us. The baby seemed calm and kept her eyes on my face for the rest of the morning.

After a few hours of teaching I wondered why Karen hadn't come in. At break time we went into the office to see if mother was OK. On the cold floor, cuddled up in a blanket, Karen lay collapsed from exhaustion.

"Shh, don't wake her. I finally got her to stop crying and to sleep," John said with the loving concern of a father. "Stace, this isn't normal is it? Are babies this much trouble?" I knew that it was a lot of work to be a mother to a new baby, but Karen's exhaustion stemmed from more than just sleep deprivation.

In the hard days that followed, I watched helplessly as Karen passed her daughter from resident to staff member—anyone who would take her for a while. I knew one of the residents who took her for an evening had AIDS. I was as naive about AIDS at the time, as about people. All I knew was that Karen's baby was being passed around like a toy. I knew, too, that the baby wasn't much better off with Karen herself. The only response Karen had ever seen to bad behavior was hitting. I knew Liza was a difficult child and that Karen slapped her out of frustration when she wouldn't stop crying. When I heard that she had dropped the baby down the stairs, I couldn't take any more. I called up my mother from work and begged her to come help this baby and her mother.

"They're both going to die if somebody doesn't."

"I'll be there in about an hour," she said.

What started as baby-sitting quickly turned into a mission of salvation. My mother met Liza and Karen and fell in love with both. She took it upon herself to be Karen's escape route, her chance at breaking the cycle of poverty and abuse. She and her family would be Karen's family and provide love, lessons in motherhood, transportation to work, whatever it took to "fix" this mother and child. Within a matter of weeks, both Karen and Liza were living with my mother and step-father, so when Karen wasn't working she could be with her child. My mother was in her late forties. Her youngest child was eight, and the stress of a hard life was beginning to show. She knew little about drug babies or drug-addicted, alcoholic mothers. Nonetheless, Karen and Liza became her sacred mission.

Liza had been badly neglected in her first two months. Besides the malnutrition, she suffered residual effects and damage from Karen's drug use during pregnancy. She cried continually and couldn't keep food down. You couldn't hold or rock this baby without her crying unless you were walking. Every hour turned into a major trauma trying to learn what help this little girl needed. Sleeping was impossible. Karen still hit the baby, too, and soon my mother never dared leave Liza and Karen alone.

Karen, herself, found for the first time in her life that she had a family—a real family that loved and accepted and supported her. My stepfather drove her back and forth to work. My mother became her mother, and her need for mothering suddenly became insatiable. Mom held and hugged her, and Karen followed her around like a puppy, always wanting more. The whole idea in inviting Karen into my mother's home was to provide her with support and give her the mothering skills she would need to take care of the baby herself. However, Karen had been so starved for love and attention as a child, she couldn't stand sharing it with her baby now. Karen said my mother was spoiling the baby, but after putting up a tough front for so long herself, it seemed she wanted to be held or loved every minute now. She threw tantrums, refusing to talk, going around the house slamming doors, and cursing at the baby's father over the telephone. He was a heavy drug user himself, and had ended up in prison during Karen's pregnancy for slashing and stabbing her and pushing her down the stairs.

All this time, Karen was going out with a drug dealer, and she spent the better parts of her days and nights high. Both my mother and I knew this—part of the plan when taking Karen in was to help her get clean and sober so she could find a job and be a good mother. My mother tried. She encouraged Karen to express her feminine side and bought Karen her first skirt. She explained over and over again proper care for the baby. We learned, though, with Karen that there are some wounds that just don't heal. Neither of us had much experience with drugs or people who were using them, and Karen's behavior was both strange and frightening. Most serious, she showed no signs of changing. She stayed high and slept, when she did, in her Levi's and high tops, ready to run, like she always had.

One night about two A.M., I got a call from Karen.

"Stacey, I need help."

"Where are you?" I said, straining through the sleep in my eyes to see the clock.

Our night together with Mel at the bar left me familiar enough with the streets to find Karen, sagged against the wall in a stairwell with a small cut bleeding on her forehead.

"Karen, what happened?" I said, while I wrapped one of her arms over my shoulder to try to help her up. She was more than a half-foot taller than I was and heavier than I'd expected.

"You've got to help me," I groaned as I strained to get this woman almost half again my size on her feet. By the time I got her home and in bed, I realized that she had simply been too drunk to find her way. In the morning, she came by the classroom to apologize. I was red-eyed and dragging from our adventure, and the kids were having a heyday teasing me about staying out too late partying the night before. She waited at the door until I took a minute to come over.

"I'm sorry about last night," she said, staring at the floor.

"Look at me," I said. She lifted her eyes, which looked worse than mine, and I had a hard time staying angry.

"You're going to make an old lady out of me," I said. Karen only nodded.

Karen was constantly apologizing, but she never did make much of an effort to change. She kept storming through my mother's house, slamming doors and cursing one minute then apologizing the next. Alcohol and drug addictions since the age of ten had left her in bad shape, and while she was living at my mother's house, she was shooting drugs into her stomach because she couldn't find a good vein in her arms or legs. Between what the drugs and drug-related infections were doing to her body, she ended up in the hospital more than once on a respirator, with no one expecting her to live.

You have to have something to sustain you in times like these, something outside yourself. For my mother, and myself, it was faith in God. Meanwhile, Karen brought us to feel and know about tragedy in a completely new way. We wanted desperately to fix her. I picked her up every time she called, day or night, and my mother put up with her tantrums and drug use, both of us full of hope and confident in the power of love alone to heal all wounds.

But what we learned from Karen was that sometimes the giving has to be enough. We wanted so badly to patch up all the damage to her life, to give her something—everything— better, but Karen wasn't helping. You can give, but someone has to take, and sometimes they don't or can't. My mother grew attached to Liza at once, problems and all. She knew this was something she was to do, that she was part of a plan to save this baby, and Liza became her passion.

We had to come to accept Liza as the issue and settle on saving her. There are people like Karen who will go through life, and maybe things will never be all right. Nothing will ever be fair. The system that couldn't help them—or, as in Karen's case, that helped destroy them—might not be able to reclaim them. But the test for us remains, the test to love unconditionally, to give, even when the giving is all there is.

42

The giving took on new dimensions, though, when Karen finally shocked my mother by begging her to take her baby. This had never been part of the plan.

"You've got to," Karen begged. She had decided to go back to living on her own. "I can't give her nothing. You've got to be her chance."

Three months later, I stood in the judge's chambers as a witness at the adoption proceedings. Five chairs sat facing a large mahogany desk. A distinguished looking man, silver hair and all, stood to greet us as we entered. Holding tightly to Karen's hand, I secretly wished she hadn't asked me to be a witness. Only the judge's questions and Karen's quiet answers broke the awkward silence. With each question, Karen squeezed harder as she answered, "Yes sir." When the judge asked if there were anything she would like to say, she spoke calmly.

"I want my daughter to know that I loved her enough to give her what I couldn't if she stayed with me." Sitting next to Karen with her hand clamped to mine, I had all but stopped breathing.

"I want her to know that's why I did this," Karen said, "because I loved her."

"That's all?" the judge asked when she didn't say anything more.

Karen nodded.

I had a new baby sister.

✄

"You'll be wanting to take every one of them home," John said to me one day toward the end of that year. We were sitting behind the counter at the office, and I was massaging my feet after a long day in new shoes.

"Not every one," I said, smiling. "I don't want Albert Serrano. That kid makes me crazy."

"It's a hard line to walk," John said. "You've got to care to come down here in the first place, and then you've got to be tough enough or get tough enough so you can stand it. You don't have enough money in your wallet or hours in the day to give to everybody who needs something, but if you get too tough, you aren't much good anymore, really."

"So what's the secret?" I asked, while I worked my feet back into the shoes for my walk to my car.

John looked at me across the desk. "You do all you can."

It's all anybody can ask. ✏

✐ LESSON PLAN ✂

Cookie Crumble

Materials: Cookies.

The lesson may work better if you have just enough cookies for each person in the classroom to have one, or not quite enough.

Object: To help students understand the difficulties, rewards, and sacrifices involved in sharing and receiving.

Activity:

- Distribute cookies unevenly among class members. Give some three, some two, some one, and some none. Tell the students not to eat their cookies before you've had a chance to discuss some things, but after your discussion they can do as they wish.

- Ask the students to describe the situation. Invite them to talk about how they feel having three or one or no cookies.

- Let the students know that this situation is in their hands. They are free to share their cookies or not share them at any time during the lesson, but they can not eat them until the lesson is over.

- Ask the students if they are going to share, and allow them to do so if and as they wish. While allowing students time to discuss the situation among themselves, encourage them to talk about what responsibility they have, if any, to share with others who have none or less than they do. Ask the students who have no cookies how it feels to be dependent upon those who have cookies.

- Ask if it is hard to share and why. Discuss how it feels to share and how it feels to receive. How much do the students stand to lose by giving? What reasons are there for sharing? How painful is it?

Close: Give the students one last chance to redistribute the cookies, if they wish. ✂

"Don't Be a Kid" Rules

In the middle of my second year, the School With No Name moved with the family shelter to a new shelter located in a renovated warehouse a little closer to town. The new shelter was clean with white hallways and blue doors, much like a college dormitory. Each small family room had a double bed, a bunk bed, and space for a crib.

The school was assigned a room on the second floor. It was four times the size of the room at the old shelter, with a sink, and new, clean carpet on part of the floor. Along one wall was a recessed area we filled with books and a soft gray couch to use as a library. East-facing windows let in the morning sunlight, and being on the second floor, we could open the windows and not see what was going on down below in the streets. We had new desks and chairs, four new chalkboards, and a separate room we could use for computers, art days, and quiet reading.

A friend of mine who used to come weekly to tutor and interact with the children at the old shelter admitted that he had more trouble feeling empathy for the kids coming into my beautiful, newly stocked classroom. I think it was a common attitude at first. The poverty and misery were always apparent at the old shelter where everything was cramped and shoddy. I did what I could to convince him that while the environment had changed, the tragedies happening to the children had not. The needs were the same, even if we were better equipped to meet some of them for the ninety days we might have a child.

Even more important than the new room, with an increase

in staff and through constant meetings required between guests and their caseworkers, the shelter was better able to keep tabs on who was meeting their children's educational needs. By this time the school was well enough established to require attendance, either at the shelter or a public school, as part of a family's being granted shelter privileges. If families had trouble making their children's education a priority, caseworkers saw to it that this was written into the contract each family made with the shelter.

As I increasingly took on the role of advocate, getting the message out that these children badly needed the district and community's assistance, doors began to open. Over the next few years, transportation was arranged for the junior high children, and while we waited for a similar arrangement at the high school, I drove those students to school and made sure they went into the building. Close contact with school administrators assured these students a more positive experience than Danny had and the extra support they needed. We made connections with resource people from other educational fields, including special education and speech therapy. When I realized I had twelve- and thirteen-year-old boys going through puberty, I called to ask for nurses to come and teach health education. When I decided that we had gifted children at the shelter school, I let the district know, and teachers trained to work with the gifted offered their services to the shelter children.

I felt something like a tiny Who on Horton the Elephant's dust speck from the Dr. Suess story, shouting, "We're here, we're here." The best chance these children would have to break the cycle of deprivation was education and connecting with adults who would nurture and mentor them. That required letting others know of the need.

Living daily with the tragedy of the children's lives and our small successes pushed me ahead. Something inside me wouldn't let me give in.

✂

It was our second winter at the new school when the two Ross brothers entered the shelter. Their shoulders slumped, their eyelids drooped, and they struggled to catch their breath as we climbed the stairs on the way to the second floor. I wondered if they'd be able to stay awake long enough to learn anything from me.

"Let's rest a minute," I suggested as we reached the landing, and they gratefully stopped. Like many of the children I teach, these boys were not in good physical condition. Their skin was not a clear, healthy color, but the mottled gray of overlooked children. They wore clothing at least two sizes too big. Their grimy tennis shoes were riddled with holes and had no laces. Alex, the smaller of the two, watched me with large, brown eyes through a mop of dark brown hair.

"You know what?" he said matter-of-factly, "I been kicked out of school lots of times for not following the rules." His tone let me know me that he expected this time would be no different.

"Oh, really?" I responded. "What kind of rules?" Seeing that I was truly interested, he warmed up to his topic.

"Oh, stupid ones like don't talk, sit still, don't bug your neighbor. You know, all the 'don't be a kid' rules."

I'd come to be more adept at recognizing important listening and teaching moments. Quietly, I nodded and agreed with Alex.

"I don't like it when I have to sit still all the time, either," I said, as we started up the stairs again. "And I'll bet you're like me, and you like to share your ideas out loud."

"Sometimes," Alex said, wiping his nose on a sleeve.

"I'll tell you what, if there's a rule at the school you don't like or don't understand, we'll talk about it, and maybe we'll change it."

He smiled at his older brother, then at me. "I like you," he said, "and your brown eyes are pretty."

"Thank you, Alex," I said. "I like yours, too."

Alex and his brother Isaac followed me into the class-room, where they sat with the other fifteen children on the rug. I introduced the Ross brothers and explained to them that we started out each day with a "jam session."

"We all sit together in a circle, and whatever you need to say, you can say it," I told them. "It never leaves the circle, and we get a chance to help each other solve our problems." I had found that the kids liked our jam sessions because they got to talk about anything and everything. This gave them a chance to help each other and to learn that they weren't alone in their fears and their worries. Sometimes we got hor-ror stories—an arrest, a drug bust, a knife fight from the night before. Sometimes stories of hope—Katie's father just landed a job; Rob's sister had her new baby. The jam ses-sions have been more valuable to me than any college course on social issues could ever dream of being for gaining firsthand an understanding of homelessness from the people it affects the most—the children.

Our jam session had a few rules: only one speaker at a time, and everybody had to be polite—no unkindness towards anybody's story if you wanted to stay in the circle. Then we ended with a "compliment circle," an opportunity to tell someone what you like about them.

"I like the colors in your sand painting, Mary."

"You look nice today, Teacher."

The room filled with good feeling as we finished, and I watched as Alex just listened wide-eyed and soaked up this new environment of kid power. Something told me he was going to benefit from our program. He was going to get a chance to express himself and grow.

After jam session, we got settled into our desks to look over the tasks planned for the day. "Let me review our pay-ment policy for our new employees," I said, turning to Alex and Isaac. "Students are the employees here at the school.

Every day you come to school and work, you get paid. English today is worth five points. Your math worksheet is worth three. You can trade the points on Fridays to spend at the school store." I unlocked the plywood cabinet so Alex and Isaac could take a look. They could buy socks, underwear, shoes, colored pencils, sketch pads. As I closed the store, I overheard Sammy lean over to Alex and whisper, "She works us hard, dude, but she's fair."

I wrote on the board each subject that we would be covering for the day, and the points to be earned as each one was completed. The kids knew exactly what was expected of them, and Alex caught on quickly. At the end of the day he stashed his writing journal and his pencil into the cubbyhole that now had his name on it, then came over to interrupt me while I was talking with a teaching assistant.

"Hey, Teach," he said loudly enough to get the attention of anybody in the room, "see you tomorrow."

✂

For the first week Alex exhibited honeymoon behavior, but as he became more comfortable, some of the tricks which had probably violated the "don't be a kid" rules at his other schools snuck out. For one thing, Alex was bright, but he was easily distracted and always more interested in what was going on at the next table than in his own work. After a good discussion following class one day, I found that a look or a few words was generally adequate to keep him working quietly with his group.

Another "trick" was a little more serious. I discovered that when my back was turned, Alex was taking food from the snack cupboard. I didn't want to embarrass him by speaking of it in front of the other students, so after school one Thursday I asked him to stay a few minutes after class.

"Alex," I said, "I'm your teacher and your friend, so I will always provide you with what you need as long as you ask me." I paused to kneel beside him. "But if you take from me when you think I'm not looking, then I feel hurt and so do the other kids."

Alex looked down. "I know, Teach, but I'm really hungry." I gathered Alex in for a hug and asked,

"Don't you eat your breakfast?"

"No," Alex shook his head.

"How come?"

Alex shrugged. The shelter provided breakfast for families between 6:30 and 8:00, but if you weren't there, you didn't eat. As Alex and I talked, I learned that his family had no alarm clock and no one else got up in time to eat, so Alex never ate breakfast. Our school lunch wasn't brought in until 12:30.

I knew I couldn't teach Alex if he was hungry, regardless of the rules. We solved the immediate problem between the two of us.

"Alex," I said, "we can work this out. Just tell me when you are hungry and I will make sure your tummy is full. OK?" He nodded, then dragged his feet as he left class as though I had grounded him to his room.

I didn't need to worry about Alex taking things too hard. He quickly became a master at working the system. He would sidle up to me with his big brown eyes looking up into mine. "Teach, I'm hungry," he would whisper, his hand caressing my arm. How could I say no?

During his entire stay, Alex was the first child through my door in the morning and the last to leave. I liked him for his drive and his enthusiasm, even though it bubbled over some-times during class and he made himself a nuisance with stunts—like trying to beat me to the phone when it rang, so he could answer it and be silly. But in time, and from the benefit of getting lots of extra warnings, he settled down to where he was a fun and manageable student—unless someone was invading his space.

One day I had the children arrange their chairs into a horseshoe. I didn't need to leave much space in between them because I was able to walk inside the half-circle to speak and interact with the kids. James sat on Alex's right, and each time James's elbow accidentally brushed against Alex it set Alex off. Although it began unintentionally, the whole thing soon escalated into a game of let's-see-how-far-I-can-push-you.

I quickly herded James and Alex into the hall to talk about it, where James explained that at first it was just accidental. Then it got funny to see Alex freak out.

Suddenly, Alex came alive. "Everyone hits me and bugs me, and tries to make me cry, and I don't like it," he yelled, his little body shaking. He had no power, no control over this part of his life, and now every nerve was lashing out against this. I sent James back into the room, while I stayed in the hallway with Alex until he calmed down. He looked so small and frustrated, I wanted to scoop him up and smother out his hurt with hugs, but something told me I had better just let him be. So I waited while he finished crying and ground his fists into his eyes to clear out the tears.

"Are you ready to go back in?" I asked quietly. He nodded and took the hand I held out to him.

When I sat down with James later and asked if he saw how upset Alex had been, he became visibly frightened, not about the possibility of getting into trouble, but because he had hurt another child so much. I had learned that like most kids, these children enjoy bugging and teasing each other, but when one of them says, "Stop. I hurt all the time," their peers swiftly become sympathetic. They know how it feels.

Later I would find out that Alex's older brothers were very rough with him and often picked on him as older brothers will. However, since his mother had left the family and his father worked long hours, Alex had no parent nearby to say, "Enough, kids. Knock it off." As the youngest, he was powerless in his own home. He could fight back, but he could never win, and he was developing a temper.

A few weeks passed without incident. Then one day Alex came in looking very despondent. I put down the papers I was marking and looked at him over my desk.

"What's up, Alex?" I asked.

With big tears filling those beautiful brown eyes, Alex told me how his older brother had hit him really hard for no reason.

"You know," Alex growled, "sometimes I just feel like killing someone, so don't be surprised if I do."

I came around the desk to put an arm around him. I didn't need to remind him that there was no fighting in class. "When it gets bad, Alex, come get me and we'll go next door and get a Coke."

His face brightened a little. "OK," he promised, "but if anyone even looks at me wrong today you better be ready to go."

"I will," I assured him.

The rest of the day he controlled his anger with great effort, and I made sure that we made frequent eye contact, reassuring one another that if things got ugly, I would leave the class with an aide, and we would head out together for a Coke. I decided that after class I would sit down with Alex and plan a reward that he could work toward and remember during hard times like today.

Along with the points they earned for completing assignments, we had come up with a system for children at the school to accumulate points for positive contributions they made toward their education or that of their peers. The system rewards the children for participating, bringing their homework back completed, and treating their peers and teachers with respect. They learn that those who work extra hard receive attention, while those who make it difficult for others to be productive don't get "paid" as well as their peers. Each child is aware of the consequences of making the workplace unproductive. No work, no pay. This way, children learn to take ownership of their own educational plan. They also learn to work as a team, to treat others with respect, and to provide safe experiences for their "co-workers."

Alex had done well with this system, but I felt he needed something more. I just didn't know what.

As the day ended, the children trailed one by one out of the classroom. All except Alex. "Notice how I kept my cool?" he asked proudly.

"I did," I said warmly. "You controlled your anger very well today. Shall we talk about a reward you can work towards for doing as well as you did today?"

Alex lit up. "I know exactly what I want, and if anyone can do it, you can." I grinned to see the master manipulator at work.

"I was thinking," he continued, "I'd really like to meet Karl Malone. You know, he's an NBA all-star basketball player for the Utah Jazz."

"Yes, of course I know who he is," I answered, frantically thinking to myself what an awesome request I was going to be asked to meet. I was still in shock when Alex spoke again.

"I heard he loves kids," Alex said hopefully.

"I'm sure he does, Alex," I stammered.

"Well, that's what I'd like best," Alex concluded. "I'd like to meet Karl Malone."

I promised I would do my best, but I felt hopeless. How could I let Alex down now that he trusted me? How could I risk such a failure when he was finally learning that kids are important people who have a legitimate need to be heard and respected—as well as learning to discipline himself? How could I approach an NBA all-star?

A volunteer group got together to write the letter asking Mr. Malone to visit the School With No Name to inspire the children to stay in school and work toward their dreams. I didn't feel that we could just ask him to come and "hang" with the kids, which is what they needed most of all.

"Do you think he'll come?" Alex asked me after we mailed the letter.

"I don't know," I said. "It's basketball season. He probably isn't even in town very much. What do you think?"

"I think he will," Alex said. "I'll bet you a Coke."

To my surprise we got a positive response. Karl Malone was really coming. It was almost impossible to get the kids to concentrate on anything else because of the excitement in the classroom the last few days before his visit, and on the morning of Karl's arrival I admitted to Alex that I was a little nervous and unsure about what we had gotten into.

Alex smiled tolerantly. "Don't worry, Teach. He's just a person like you and me." I don't think Alex realized that he was absolutely right.

When Karl Malone walked in, all six-feet-nine of him, Alex's big, brown eyes got even bigger. "Wow!" he whispered to me, "he's awesome."

When I felt Karl Malone's warmth, I let him know that we wouldn't hold him to his commitment of a "stay in school" speech. Karl was thrilled. He just wanted to sit down on the floor and play with the children as if he were Uncle Karl, coming over to see all the nieces and nephews. The children bombarded him with questions. They got out rulers and measured his feet, legs, and arms. Then Alex ran his fingers through Karl's hair and mustache and felt his skin. I began to panic a little.

"Kids, be careful. Give Karl some space," I said.

"Hey, it's OK," he reassured me. "Relax." I could see then that the children brought him as much joy as he brought them. As I watched the children playing with Karl, I leaned against the bookshelf next to Karl's press secretary, both of us fighting to keep our composure and a little bit embarrassed about getting teary. Alex would never forget this reward. Meanwhile, Karl kept saying to the kids, "Hey you guys, I want you to come and watch me play ball. You can come to any game you want to."

Everyone decided quickly on Thursday, the next night,

to give them just enough time to get permission from their parents.

"Teach, can we go, can we go?" they clamored.

"Absolutely," I said. "We'll be there tomorrow night."

We went to the ball game early and had time to go down on the court to meet the other players and shake hands. Karl introduced the children as his friends, and the kids went wild in the stands all night. All we heard for the next week at school was Karl Malone and basketball. The kids were wadding up every piece of scrap paper in sight to jump shoot and slam dunk into the garbage cans and begging to have a backboard put up on the cement playground area, even though it was buried in snow, so they could "shoot some hoop."

To both Alex's and my surprise the rewards and sharing of love were just beginning. Christmas was rapidly approaching. Christmas at the shelter is different from the Christmas many families know. How does Santa know where to come if you just checked into a homeless shelter? But this year Santa was replaced by none other than "the Mailman," Karl Malone.

"Karl wants to take you all to a toy store," I announced to the kids. "He wants to get you something for Christmas."

As the kids finished shrieking with delight, Alex gasped, "He cares about us, don't he?"

"Yes he does, Alex," I said. "He sure does."

To say the children couldn't wait for the day to come gives them credit for more patience than they had. I had thought that taking my own two children Christmas shopping was overwhelming, but twenty kids? The day of the shopping trip, the children were running around the store, jumping and grabbing and looking all at once. I heard myself endlessly repeating phrases like "be polite," "remember the budget we discussed," "say 'thank-you.'" I wanted this to be a "teaching moment." Finally Karl had had enough.

"Leave them alone," he said. "You stand over there and just enjoy this." He grinned, and I grinned back. I certainly didn't want to take any joy away from Karl, who was wandering happily up and down the aisles enjoying the toys and the children. At the end of this Christmas magic I had no doubt lives would be changed forever on both sides, Mr. Malone's and those of these homeless children.

※

Christmas passed and Alex's family was able to get into a home through his father's efforts with a program that trained men and women in practical construction skills such as plumbing, wiring, and painting. If you made it all the way through the course, you got the chance to work on a house for your own family. Alex's father had come out of the program an electrician's assistant, and though the demands of his job kept him from being around much to give his boys time and supervision, he worked hard to meet his family's needs. Alex attended his neighborhood school, but every once in a while he would come to the shelter to say hi.

"Karl been back?" he would always ask.

"No," I told him one day early in May. "I did speak to him on the phone, though, and he wants you to come to his basketball camp."

"For reals?" screamed Alex. "He must have thought I was real bad."

"For reals," I assured him.

June couldn't come quickly enough for Alex that year. He became a regular at the shelter in the weeks before the camp, checking to make sure I remembered the date and that I had volunteered to take him. I picked him up at 7:15 on the first morning of the camp so that we would be sure to be there on time. He talked my ear off all the way there and forgot to unbuckle his seat belt before trying to get out of the car.

As I sat on the bleachers representing Alex's "mom," I couldn't help but compare Alex to the other children. Most of them were well dressed, right down to their name-brand basketball shoes. In contrast to Alex, they looked healthy and confident. Alex's health had improved in the time I had known him; his eyes were bright and his skin clear. But his hair hung in his eyes and his clothes and tennis shoes were hand-me-downs from his older brothers. His shorts, borrowed from his eighteen-year-old brother, threatened to fall right to his ankles with a sudden move.

This vision broke my heart. Was this a dreadful mistake? I suddenly wondered. I didn't think that Alex could suffer anymore hard knocks in life.

As I sat there in sudden despair, Karl began to sternly read the rules of the camp, which did nothing to soothe my already anxious mind.

The first rule: *Your shirt must be clean every day without fail.*
Now who's going to take care of that? I wondered. Alex's family didn't have money for extra trips to the laundromat.

The second rule: *When addressed, you will respond with "yes, sir" or "no, sir." Players who forget will run laps.*

As the rules were read, Alex looked at me. He had struggled with rules ever since I had known him, and despite the relationship we had developed over time, he still resisted rules, especially if he didn't understand *why*. To him, this would be another case of "big people" handing down "don't be a kid" rules for no good reason that he could see.

I motioned to Alex to just pay attention, we'd talk about the rules later. As we drove home that day we discussed about demanding respect and earning respect. "Not all people understand that it takes time to build trust and more than one week to build respect," I said. "Just be you and be polite. You'll be fine."

The next morning, Alex was petrified. He had to wear a shirt with a big chocolate stain on the front—it was that or none at all—and he knew he was going to have to run laps.

"Don't worry," I told him.

As we arrived at the camp, I steeled my nerve, found Karl, and took him aside. "Alex may not always have a clean shirt," I told him. "And he hasn't had the background that many of the children have. Respect for rules is harder for him than others." I asked him please not to single Alex out and humiliate him. He had had enough setbacks in life.

"You'll be sorry if you do," I said, though I said it with a sweet smile on my face, "and you'll have me to answer to." He laughed and put an arm around my shoulder.

"Don't worry, I'll make sure he's OK." I walked away relieved knowing that we both wanted him to experience this small success. By the end of the day, Alex had a new shirt Karl had provided for him

Every morning of the camp, I drove Alex there, determined to help him work with the rules and to save him from any possible humiliation. For every minute you were late, you ran a lap in front of the other children. If your shirt was dirty or untucked, that was another lap as an example so that the other kids could see that you chose to break the rules.

Alex faced other difficulties as well. It soon became apparent that the other kids were more competent at handling the ball. Though he tried his best, the other kids didn't trust him to carry it down the court. This frustrated Alex, who understood that he wasn't as skilled as they were. But because of his experiences with poverty and homelessness, Alex was a survivor. He didn't have the finesse or polish of some of the other kids, but he made his presence known and demanded to participate. He had an incredible hunger for that ball, a drive that came from a lifetime lack of opportunity, and he was an aggressive player. His hands flew all over the place as he yelled, "Throw me the ball, throw me the ball. Let me shoot it." At first, the other kids ignored him and played around him. But he kept it up for the entire week of the camp.

Aside from a few scuffles with other children, Alex worked hard and never complained. He was doing fine. While I drove him home, he would share with me the finer points of offense and defense he had picked up that morning.

Together we made goals for how many points he would score the next day, how many passes he would make, and how he would improve his teamwork and sportsmanship.

One day, halfway through the camp, I came early to pick Alex up so I could watch him play a bit before I took him home. His coach approached me as I walked in.

What now? I thought.

Alex had gotten a little "too aggressive" his coach said. I explained Alex's territory problem.

"He doesn't like to be touched or bumped," I said. I described some of Alex's background—that he didn't have a mom, that he was raised with men as the baby of the family. He had been picked on a lot and had very little cuddling; he put up his defenses, but he was very hungry for the right kind of touch.

Then Alex's coach said with great compassion, "He's definitely different. I talked about him all night to my wife. He's the kind of kid you just want to bring home." We were watching Alex out on the floor, calmed down a bit after taking his laps, but still yelling to get his hands on the ball.

"What can I do?" his coach asked, looking to help him.

"He really hasn't been talked to enough," I offered. "Just yelled at. If you get down at his level to explain things, he's a good listener." The coach nodded with new understanding and returned to the court. I looked over later to see him on one knee beside Alex, talking to him, listening, nodding his head. I could see Alex warming up to him. I don't make a habit of kissing strange men, but I could have run out and planted one on Alex's coach right then. That night Alex told me he thought his coach was one of the coolest people he'd ever met.

On Thursday, the second to the last day of camp, I stood in the doorway of the gym feeling like a proud mom. At the same time I was hurting from the scene before me. The kids were playing, and Alex kept screaming for the ball but the kids still weren't passing it to him. I could feel the tears warm my cheeks, and when I realized I was crying I quickly left before he could see me. I waited in the bathroom until I could control my emotions. Alex taught me a valuable lesson that day. Be tough, be counted, and never give up.

When it was time to leave, I stopped to buy a few of the autographed shirts Karl's staff was selling for the kids. As I was walking out Karl stopped me.

"How's he doing out there?" he said.

"He's a fighter," I told him. Then Karl quietly handed me several bills.

"Please go buy Alex some new shoes and get him a haircut," Karl said. "He'll want to look sharp for the awards ceremony."

"Thank you," I said, determined not to bawl in front of Karl Malone.

"Now, buy the brand I represent!" he added, half joking. Alex was thrilled and on the way home we stopped at a sporting goods store to buy shoes.

"It would be nice if you bought Karl's brand," I said, but when we looked over the table holding that particular brand, Alex pulled a face as he poked the shoes.

"Too girly. Not cool," he said.

Finally, he spotted a pair of plain black ones. They weren't Karl's brand, but I didn't think he would hold us to his words.

"Oh, I like these," Alex held them out for inspection. "I know they're not Karl's, but I like 'em."

The selection at the store was pretty limited, and I had to agree that the pair Alex was holding hopefully in his hands was indeed "way cool."

"I'll tell Karl they just had 'girly' colors in his brand," he promised. We laughed over his purchase, Alex happy to have the shoes and me pleased with his power to make the decision. They were his new shoes, and he was proud of them.

When I dropped Alex off at home, I gave his father ten dollars to get Alex a haircut.

"He'll be ready for you tomorrow," his father assured me.

The next morning I was surprised to see Alex walk toward the car, his head hanging in shame. His father had shaved his head himself to save the ten dollars.

I told Alex it didn't look too bad and I consoled myself by thinking that it was his last day. He'd never have to see the other kids again.

Alex's coach was waiting for him inside the door as we walked in. "Come here, Alex," he called. Alex followed him into the locker room where his coach showed him a set of brand new clothes. Alex quickly showered and came out beaming in his new clothes, his problem haircut forgotten.

"I look good, don't I?" he declared.

"You certainly do," I agreed.

For the awards ceremony, the children were seated according to their teams on the gym floor, while the proud parents sat behind them on the bleachers with cameras ready. Awards were given to kids who showed the most improvement, who had the best attitude, who showed the greatest hustle on the court. I know that Alex was not counting on receiving an award because he was bugging the kid next to him. When his name was called out as the child who had shown exemplary skills in not giving up, learning, and improving, he looked at me in complete astonishment.

He pointed to himself and I motioned, "Yes, you, Alex. Get up." He ran up to the podium to accept his certificate, beaming at the sound of applause.

I took Alex out for a late breakfast to celebrate, and as I sat across the table from him, listening to him recount his exploits of the last week, I knew this would be an experience that Alex would never forget, one that might shape him and influence choices he made later. He never did get kicked out of the School With No Name for not obeying all the "don't be a kid" rules. This gave him the chance to learn a number of things from the school and his experience with Karl, including what some of the rules were for and how they can work for you. He got to learn that if you work hard you get paid, that honesty can bring greater rewards than theft. Most important, he learned that there are people in this world who love kids, no matter how they look or where they live—even if they sometimes break the rules. ✏

Untitled

I miss my cuddles
His fur looked like the dark
sky at night.

He plays ball with me, chasing
acting like it is a mouse.

His eyes were as blue as
the sky.

—Third-grade student

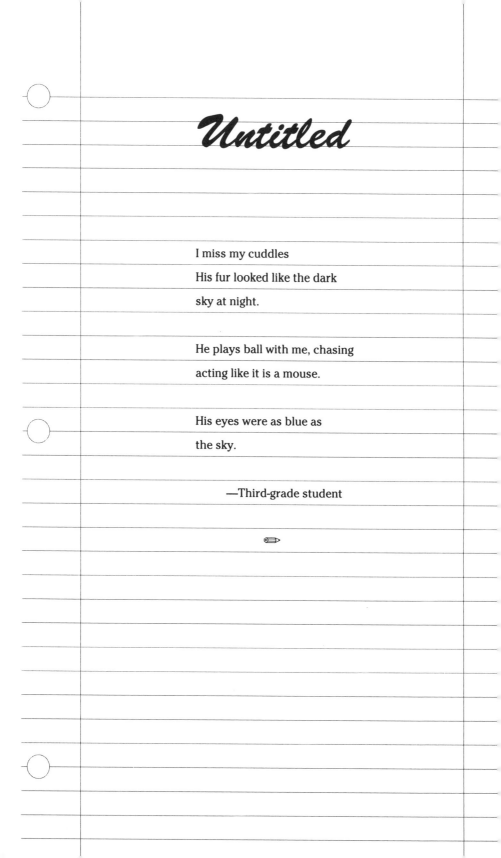

What Dana Gave

Nine-year-old Dana was another Christmas story. She pouted into the classroom one November day with her seven-year-old brother, Jesse, in tow. They had moved into the family shelter with their father the night before. Head hanging, eyes on the floor, Dana held tightly to her brother's hand while she led him to a seat then slunk into her own. She sat slumped in her chair the rest of the day, mute and unresponsive, speaking only when she couldn't answer with a nod.

During her first week at the school, Dana hid behind her tousled mop of brownish-red hair, unwilling to lift her head for even a moment to look at me. As the din and chaos of the classroom swirled around her, she sat unmoving and unwilling to participate, everything about her announcing: "I'm powerless. I'm nobody." I felt a strange affinity with this wounded child and made a pact with myself to break through her protective wall of isolation and help her see who she was—but at first it seemed that Dana's wall was made of steel. She refused to be reached. I knew this because every time I tried, I failed. Like I did on the day I tried to invite her to play Scrabble.

Jared was in the fourth grade with Dana, and we had been battling all morning over his spelling test.

"Would you like my help?" I teased placing my cold hands on his cheeks. "I'd be glad to do a dance for you or sing. Would a spoonful of sugar make the medicine go down?" I danced, I pranced, I belted out my song. The boys at Jared's table laughed. Dana did nothing. Jared's eyes opened wide. He giggled, blushed, and finally begged me to quit.

"You can't spell, neither," he retorted. He was half right. Spelling wasn't always my strong suit, and the kids loved catching my mistakes on the board. I told them it was something we could work on together, and I figured if they could catch the misspelled words, at least it meant they were learning something.

"I can spell better than you," I challenged.

"Nah," Jared said, folding his arms and leaning back in his chair. His buddies hooted and egged him on. It was time to bring out the big guns.

"All right," I said, digging for the Scrabble game in the cupboard, "bring your butt over here so I can kick it."

I was on a roll, and while the boys set up the Scrabble game, I thought I would invite Dana to play. I reached out to brush the strands of hair out of her eyes. "Can you see under there?" I teased. Gently, I placed a finger under Dana's chin, tipped her head up, and looked into huge blue eyes grown round with terror as she jerked back as though I were going to strike her. I quickly dropped my hands to my side and knelt down beside her. "It's okay," I said. "You don't have to look at me." I backed off and watched from a distance as she finished her spelling test. Nobody else in the class looked up or noticed.

Because Dana wasn't cute, cuddly, or even attractive, both adults and peers found it easy to ignore her. She moped around on the sidelines of every activity, lonely and withdrawn. She interacted with the other children only when they made fun of her, and then her only defense was tears. Tears had been my recourse, too, when anything went wrong in my growing up years. For the longest time, I would stand and cry rather than fight. I ached for her, remembering this, and I became more passionately determined to reach out to the child behind the wall.

After several frustrating days spent trying to get past the ratty hair hanging in her eyes and her refusal to talk, I finally came up with an idea. "Can you come in early tomorrow?" I asked Dana as she was leading her brother out of the classroom. Dana didn't talk, but I knew she listened and seemed to be in the habit of doing what she was asked. She nodded without looking at me. "Good," I said. "Wash your hair before you come."

The next morning at eight-thirty, Dana stood in my doorway in a grungy, lime-green t-shirt and baggy corduroy pants, rolled up so they wouldn't drag on the floor. Her hair, clean for the first time since I'd known her, hung in damp tangles.

"I found something for you that I think is really cool," I said, motioning for her to come in, "something that will make you gorgeous and help you see to do your work." I reached into my purse and came up with a hairbrush in one hand and a marbled-green headband in the other.

Dana sat stiffly while I carefully tugged through the snarled layers as best I could. Her ragged, home-barbered hair was thick and hung unevenly around her freckled neck and ears. I made some small talk, mostly to myself, and breathed in the clean scent of shampoo as I sat behind her. Dana was living with her father now, and I wondered how long it had been since she had had a mother to sit and talk with while she brushed her daughter's hair. After I finished and slipped the headband behind her ears to gather the hair out of her eyes, we searched through the science drawer and found a mirror.

"Don't you look way cool," I grinned. Dana's eyes locked on her own image in the mirror, which reflected a rare, genuine smile.

✂

With me reminding her, Dana came in before school most mornings after that, and I would brush her hair, until she was confident enough and willing to do it herself. It was a start—a little step toward the goal of helping Dana to have pride in who she was, to hold her head up. I wanted her to feel good enough about herself that she could look at me, talk to me, and face her peers with some degree of confidence. When Dana could value herself, the biggest barrier to love and learning would be overcome.

"Why don't you stay and talk for a while while I clean up?" I invited one afternoon while she headed out the door.

Startled, she looked up and asked in amazement, "How come?"

I shrugged. "Just to talk. What do you usually do after school?"

"Nothing," she glumly retorted. "We can't go outside. It's too cold, and Dad says it's too dangerous." I couldn't argue with her there, but I invited her to keep me company after class whenever she wanted.

I knew that her wall was beginning to crumble when Dana began hanging around after school to talk to me on her own. When she learned that I had a daughter, Nichole, who was just a little older than she was, Nichole became one of Dana's favorite subjects. With her newfound courage, she would often pepper me with questions. "Does Nichole have homework? Do you help her with it? Does she like having a mom who's a teacher?"

Laughing at her sudden inquisitiveness I responded, "Sometimes she doesn't like me reminding her about homework when she has so many other things she wants to do. She's busy all the time."

"Like with swimming lessons and student council?" Dana said, details she had stored away from earlier conversations.

"You have a good memory," I said, while I took the books Dana handed me and slipped them into place on a shelf.

"I wish you were my mom," Dana sighed. "And you could help me do homework." The longing in her voice surprised me, though not as much as when she took my hand, held it tightly, and wouldn't let go for some time.

✂

Just when I began seeing a lot of progress with Dana, December came and I had much less time to devote to her. *Overwhelming* doesn't begin to describe the Christmas season at the shelter. It hits us like a tidal wave, causing panic and frustration; and we are inevitably knocked for a loop by the whole range of emotions left in its wake.

The pressing awareness of the differences between the *haves* and the *have nots* settles on us like a gloomy cloud, dimming the glow of this bright season. At the shelter school we unwrap all gifts before they are assigned to the children in order to avoid the problem of well-wishers providing worn-out toys, even used pencils and crayons, as gifts. An obviously used toy from Santa just doesn't cut it, no matter how poor you are. It makes yet another statement to the children that they are worth less than someone else. In addition to making sure all the shelter children are taken care of, we also try to set aside gifts to share with children who have just left or those who come in after the holidays with the heartbreaking announcement: "We didn't get anything for Christmas because we were living in our car."

The year that Dana and her brother, Jesse, were at the shelter was the year of the Santa Claus train. Santa was coming by train into the station just down the street with gifts for the underprivileged children. On the morning he was to make his appearance, the announcement blared over the intercom: "Santa will arrive at 10:00 A.M." The children cheered.

"Teacher, isn't it time to go?" Jesse pleaded. Dana looked up, brushing her hair out of those big blue eyes open wide with excitement.

"He won't be here for another hour," I explained, but reason was useless. The whole class fidgeted and griped until we finally gave in. We got the twenty-or-so children paired up, rounded up some parents to help chaperone, and walked the two blocks to the station in the bright December daylight.

The train station rang with the chatter and shouts of

dozens of children as we zigzagged through the crowd. With impatience and anticipation bursting from them in giggles, the shelter children shifted from one foot to the other, but managed to be generally polite as they waited for their turn on Santa's knee. A convincing Santa with a real beard talked to each one then handed each a wrapped gift. *This was Christmas,* I thought. I was as excited as the rest of them and ordered every one of the children to bring their presents after they opened them to show me.

Dana tore the red ribbon and green paper off her present then paused and slowly lifted a Barbie bed out of a box. Her face fell. With her eyes on the ground, dragging her feet, she wove her way through the other children until she got back to me. I asked her what Santa had given her. Without looking up, she held the bed up to show me. She didn't say a word, but she didn't have to. I knew she didn't have a Barbie, and I knew she knew her father had no money to buy one.

My heart sunk down into my shoes. Suddenly the station was just noisy and crowded; all the cheer was gone. Unable to find words, I put my arm around Dana and held her tightly, wondering where Jesse was. I spied him opening a battery-operated toy. Pulling it out of the box he tried to get it to work. He drew his lips together in a tight line and squinted his eyes. Finally Jesse realized the toy needed batteries, but there were no batteries in the package. He bravely fought to hold back the tears. So did I, but it was no use. They started rolling down my face. Nobody had meant to be unkind when they gave their gifts. Who ever remembers to buy the batteries? But people who have never been in a situation of deprivation sometimes don't recognize how many toys can be useless in the vacuum of poverty.

I had plenty of kids at the school who toted their Walkmans around and always had spare change for video games or a yellow canister of the nasty chili spices my sixth-grade boys bought at the Mexican store as a snack.

Dana and Jesse weren't part of this group. I could feel the old indignation stirring in me. Some kids couldn't get a break, not even at Christmas.

As I stood there feeling helpless, angry, and unbearably sad, a professional-looking woman approached me and inquired kindly, "Are you here with the children?"

"I teach some of them at the homeless shelter," I replied.

"I'm a reporter, here for the train," she explained.

We began comparing notes. I explained Dana and Jesse's predicament, and we shared a bittersweet moment of oneness, as I found out this reporter had been noticing the same disappointments.

"Everybody means well," I said. "They just don't always understand what it's like."

"Here," my reporter friend said, reaching in her purse. Her cheeks were as wet as mine now. "Please go buy batteries, or anything the children need." That tender moment was the beginning of a wonderful friendship between us and proved a bright spot in Dana and Jesse's Christmas.

✂

As the Christmas chaos wore on, Dana faded into the background, quietly observing while the schoolroom became a bustling clearinghouse filled with gifts and treats to be sorted and distributed as fairly and sensitively as possible—no easy task. The visitors and calls from local businesses and civic groups wanting to provide parties and receive an updated wish list for the children came nonstop. I loved this aspect of the Christmas season. I loved the people who gave. We never wanted to turn the community away, because they are a vital resource to the children, but I did find myself more than once wanting to shout, "Just leave me alone for a while so I can teach!"

Always, the children were in the middle. One day after visitors had filed in and out all morning, David burst out in exasperation, "I feel like a fish in a fishbowl, and everybody is looking in to see what a homeless kid looks like. I'm not a fish, I'm just a person."

"You're right, David, you're not a fish," I assured him.

Dustin giggled in response, "It's like we're animals in the zoo." Then he and Monroe went to work making signs that said, "Feed me, I do tricks."

Although I had little extra time to concentrate on Dana, I did notice that she always made sure her little brother got his treat or gift before she got her own. She was extremely protective of Jesse, and fussed over him constantly. One day in the middle of December, Dana waited for my answer as Jesse asked me fearfully, "How will Santa know I live in a shelter?" Suddenly every child at the first- and second-grade tables was all eyes and ears.

"Santa is magic, Jesse, he knows who you are and where you live," I assured him, floundering in my own faith in a society that forced a child to grow up so fast he couldn't experience the magic of Santa Claus. Judging from the quiet around Jesse's table, a little more assurance was in order. To make doubly sure St. Nick knew *these* children's whereabouts, for our writing project that afternoon we wrote letters to Santa. A few minutes into the exercise, I walked up behind Jesse, who was showing his sister what he had written:

"I HOPE YU DUN'T KARE THAT WE AR HOMLES."

"He likes us anyway," Dana declared in a somber voice. "Don't he teacher?" she asked, looking up at me for reassurance with hopeful eyes. I nodded.

"All children are important to Santa, Dana. No matter where they live."

Aaron, a third grader whose family had been at the shelter before, interrupted, "What's the use of writing a letter? Santa never comes, and if he did he wouldn't get us what we want anyway."

When Dana saw the look of distress on Jesse's face, she whispered to him, "*He* doesn't know."

Jesse seemed satisfied and went back to work on his letter, pausing only to ask how to spell Nintendo.

In reality, Santa *would* come to the children in the shelter, as he had every year I had worked at the School With No Name, because of the generosity of so many people in the community. The shelter families are grateful for the help, but no matter how destitute they are, it is not easy to be on the receiving end. When they lose self-reliance, their sense of pride and self-worth is shaken; they experience conflicting feelings of gratitude and resentment, hope and self-doubt, expectation and humiliation. The painful question, "What's wrong with me that I can't take care of my own family?" surfaces over and over again. Organizations who want the media to cover their generosity add the shadow of public scrutiny and pity to the shelter families' own introspection. Year after year the whole scenario leaves me torn between gratitude and guilt for the comfort and abundance I go home to each night. When the holidays are over, I am usually ready for them to end.

Two days before Christmas break that year, Dana overheard me discussing with the other teachers my upcoming visit to the hospital for radiation treatment. I had been diagnosed with cancer toward the end of my first term teaching at the school. I'd shared the experience with the children. As a class, we discussed disease, hospitals, and being afraid. And they had unleashed their love on me in a torrent of get-well cards, hugs, tears, and predictions for my speedy recovery. My last surgery for thyroid cancer had been a couple of years ago, but I was going in over Christmas vacation for another series of treatments to kill any active tissue that might still be growing. *Cancer* is a scary word and I didn't want Dana to be frightened, so I explained to her about my previous surgeries then showed her the scar on my neck. She reached up and softly ran her finger along the scar.

"When they cut into your neck did it feel like your head was comin' off?" she asked.

"I was asleep, silly," I laughed, "so I really didn't feel anything."

"Were you very scared?" she asked next, peering closely at my neck.

"When they first told me I had cancer, I was frightened," I said honestly. "I didn't know a lot about this kind of cancer."

Immediately she jumped in, "Were you afraid you were gonna die?"

"Only at first," I said. "I was lucky that it was a very slow growing cancer and the doctors found out about it early."

"I was afraid I would die once," Dana almost whispered, forgetting for a moment to stay behind that protective wall.

"When was that?" I asked. I didn't know much about Dana's past, only that she and her brother now lived with their father, although custody had originally been granted to the mother. Instead of answering me, Dana changed the subject.

"Are you coming back?" she asked with real concern in her voice.

"I'll be back," I promised. This sad child seemed to have an uncanny understanding of fear and pain, but where had it come from?

The following day I was preparing to close the school down for Christmas break. As the children made a mad rush for the door I sighed with relief—I had made it through another holiday season. Working at my desk, I noticed Dana still milling around the room; good-byes are hard for the kids, and I assumed Dana wanted a private one. After she was sure the classroom would stay empty, Dana made her way to the front of the room, hiding something behind her back.

"Are you going to the hospital soon?" she asked, still keeping her hands behind her.

"Yes," I said.

"Are you scared?"

"Not particularly," I answered, not really looking at her, my hands and eyes still occupied with clearing my desk. "I've gone there before and I know what to expect."

She stood watching for a minute, then pressed me harder, "I want to know *really* if you're afraid to go the hospital." I stopped to ponder what she was saying and I finally gave her my full attention.

"Yes," I said, "I'm a little afraid. I don't want to be sick anymore."

"Is Nichole afraid?" Dana intently probed, not knowing that she had struck a tender spot. The possibility that I wouldn't be around to watch my children grow was, in fact, my greatest fear, and my eyes began to fill with tears.

Dana placed her gift on my desk and took a step back. "I have something that will help you," she said. "Something" was a black-and-white stuffed bear.

"This is Bear and he's my friend. He'll go with you to the hospital, and when your tummy starts to hurt, squeeze him. It helps to hold him tight when you're afraid. It really works," she promised.

Speechless, I watched as she presented a second gift.

"Do you know who this is?" she asked as she held a picture toward me.

I nodded.

"Who?" she questioned.

"Jesus."

"That's right," she said. "When I've been scared, he's helped me, and he'll help you too. You can put him on your mirror, and when it gets really bad you can ask him to help you feel better. He'll whisper in your ear, 'It's okay, Stacey, it's almost over.'"

Totally overcome, I couldn't speak, but opened my arms to her, and she shyly returned my embrace. All the warmth, all the love of the holiday season seemed to gather around the two of us in that room. I doubt I have ever been given more meaningful gifts; how this wounded little person could so powerfully reach out to my small need when her own was so great, I couldn't begin to fathom.

"Thank you, Dana," was all I finally choked out.

During the next few weeks, I found myself squeezing Bear quite regularly. Every time I did, I thought of Dana. I was amazed at the love and strength of this little nine-year-old child, yet I still wondered what experiences had left her with such wisdom and empathy. When I got back to work, I became obsessed with learning more about her background. What I learned made her gifts even more precious.

Not long before I met Dana, the sheriff in a small town in another state had received an anonymous phone call from a worried woman who said she hadn't seen the neighbor children in days. When the sheriff and a deputy knocked on the door, they discovered Dana's mother and her boyfriend. The couple first claimed that the children were visiting an aunt, but the officers played a hunch and pressed them with questions until the mother admitted that the children were locked in the cellar. The boyfriend insisted the children were fine, they had simply been "bad" and needed to be "punished." The sheriff descended the stairs into an unlit, windowless room to find Dana and her brother crouched in a corner on the damp, dirt floor. They had been given no food or water and were very weak. With one hand, the little girl was holding onto her brother, and in the other she clutched a dirty, black-and-white stuffed bear.

I still have Dana's "Bear," and her picture of Jesus is hanging on my mirror. Now and then, when I am tired and wonder where I can get the strength to face another day or reach out to yet another child, I squeeze Bear and I can hear Dana's childish voice promising me that the fear and the pain will go away. With her gift, Dana gave me more than a picture and a bear. She also shared a portion of her innocent

child's faith in the gentle voice of a higher power that comforted her during those dark days locked in the cellar—the
voice that whispered, "It's OK, Dana, it's almost over." ▱

All That Can Be Yours

Math was first on the agenda the day Jenny called me at the shelter. I had begun a fun lesson I had been using for a couple of years. Each child received a bag of M&M's and a list of problems that related to the colors of M&M's. We would add, subtract, classify the candies by color, and create story problems that encouraged sharing. Then we could finish math with a snack. As I began to introduce the lesson that morning, the phone rang. I was the only adult in the room so I quickly picked it up.

"Stacey?" a breathy, female voice on the other end of the line said.

"Yes, this is Stacey," I said.

"Stace, it's Jenny." My heart raced.

"How are you, Hon?"

"I don't have much time but I thought I should tell you before someone else does," Jenny said. "I'm going to have a baby." I felt my stomach drop like someone had opened a trapdoor. There was a long silence before I could speak. Out of the corner of my eye I saw a handful of M & M's flying through the air aimed right at the fourth graders' table. Warfare.

"Jenny, are you all right?" I felt panic surge through me. Jenny was still just a child, only fifteen. "Let me come and get you."

"No," she replied, "everything's okay. I just thought you should know. I'm not having an abortion, but I haven't decided if I should raise it or not." I wanted to give her some counsel, but I had no prepared speech or sure-fire advice for unexpected pregnancies. I knew that strong-willed Jenny would do whatever she felt she had to do, in any case.

"Keep in touch. Let me know how you are," I urged her. "And remember I love you." After the call, I stood a moment without moving and gave a silent prayer while the class descended into anarchy around me. "Please, God, go with her. Help her to remember all those talks we had. Help her to make good choices."

I was no stranger to the fear that Jenny was to face. I remember the terrifying reality that a child was growing inside of me at the age of sixteen. I was drowning in a swirl of hopelessness and fear, with my hopes and dreams shattered, but I can remember my mother's words when I broke the news to her.

"I love you, Stacey. Just come home and we'll work this out." I had Greg, too, who insisted he was madly in love with me and would never leave me or his child. He had gone on insisting the same thing now for ten years. He was the grounded person in our relationship, always calm and realistic, and he always believed in me. I wondered if Jenny would receive any of the support that I had been given.

But at the moment, I had twenty pairs of eyes watching me and wondering how I was going to respond to the hundreds of M&M's all over the floor. I left the phone and glared at my third graders who had started the M&M fight.

"I'll count to five," I said, putting on my best stern face. "At five I'll see every single M&M off the floor and into the garbage." They scrambled at the warning. I didn't even tell them it was gross when they stuffed handfuls into their mouths, chewing quickly then swallowing, unable to bear throwing the treats away.

✂

Jenny had come along early in my career. She didn't fit my young and naive stereotype of what a homeless child should be. Her silky, black hair hung past her shoulders, and she carried herself with an air of confidence and style, even for an eleven-year-old. She wasn't sluggish or out of shape as so many of the school children were. She smiled easily and danced when walking would do.

Jenny and I became instant pals. Her energy and love for learning filled me up, and her innovations in my classroom proved invaluable. Being a new teacher, I had no idea how I was going to handle thirty children from grades kindergarten to six. With that many students in my little classroom, there were just not enough desks for each child. Jenny told me she'd be right back; then she went out and gathered nightstands from the trailers so that each child would have something to write on. As the children worked, she walked up and down the aisles and tapped each paper. "That's a beautiful A," she'd say to one child, or "You do that so well" to another.

When the class got so large that it became completely unmanageable, Jenny went to the shelter dayroom and recruited mothers. "My teacher needs help," she told them. When no one was quick to respond, she took one of the women who had a little boy in the class by the hand.

"Come on," she urged.

"I don't know nothing about being a teacher," the reluctant mother responded.

"You just need to sit with Davy while he does his worksheet. You, too," Jenny said over her shoulder to another mother who had three daughters between kindergarten and the third grade at the school. Jenny hauled them in and sat them at two different tables where groups of five or six children were gathered and supposed to be filling out worksheets on everything from colors to the parts of speech. I heard Davy shouting, "Where does yellow go?" and his mother saying, "You show me." Jenny introduced me to the fact that the mothers and fathers of my students were often as hungry to regain their childhood as their children were to experience it in the first place. It was the beginning of a very long and loving relationship between the shelter school and the parents.

Watching Jenny work with the children and the parents at the shelter gave me a better understanding of our purpose at the school. The focus on academics became secondary—love of learning was primary. If I couldn't teach the parents to value education, then the love of learning I was trying to teach the children would not be kept alive after they left me. And if I were ever going to understand the parents, walk in their shoes and get rid of my stereotypes about how they had gotten where they were, if I were ever going to understand their plight, I couldn't be timid—dipping my toes in the cold water of their world and quickly pulling back. I needed to listen to them and learn from them. Jenny encouraged me to take the plunge. "Go talk to Amy's mother about her," she would say. Or, "Don't you know Lois?"

So, one day after class, instead of hurrying home I took a deep breath and walked into the dayroom, where the mothers congregated with their children. All eyes focused on me as I began to speak, "I thought I'd say hi before heading home to face the mob."

Two mothers shifted over to make a place for me on the filthy couch and I sat down beside them.

"I'm Lois, Ted's mother." I shook her hand, which was chapped and rough from the harsh weather.

"I'm Connie. You got my Jackie in there. How's she doing? I worry because she's been out of school for months. I hope you can help her."

"Jackie's a great kid," I responded. "She just needs a little confidence. Give her some time. She'll be fine."

Connie handed me half her sandwich.

"Eat this, honey. You're too thin. If you're gonna keep up with our kids you gotta eat." I stared at the food I knew I didn't want to touch, much less eat.

"Thanks," I said with a sigh as I took the sandwich, "I'm starving."

Each night after school for those few months, no matter how exhausted I was, I took some time to drop in at the day-room, say hi, share a candy bar, drink a Coke, and talk. Jenny would come with me sometimes and give the mothers an animated recap of the day's events, always making a big deal of their children's accomplishments. She knew everybody's name, who belonged to whom. With Jenny at my side, the parents learned to trust me as I held their babies, changed diapers, sat with the mothers, and talked with the fathers about the job market, the economy, and hobbies in which we shared some common interest.

These were the most unusual parent-teacher conferences I could ever have imagined, yet the bond that was being created gave both the children and me the parental support we so desperately needed. Our talks confirmed my underlying conviction that all people—regardless of economics or environment—hope, hurt, and worry about essentially the same things.

As we watched the children play one Tuesday during recess, Margy, Jason's mother, smoked a cigarette and shared with me a lesson that I have never forgotten as we sat on the cement curb.

"My old man and old lady, they were both alcoholics," she said, resting her arms that were skinny as chicken bones on her knees. "We never knew when we were gonna have a meal 'cause all the money went for booze. I was the oldest, and my little brothers and sisters would be hangin' on me, cryin' to eat. I'd go to my mama and say to her, 'The kids are hungry,' and she'd tell me, 'You know we only eat one meal a day around here. I got no money.' Then she and the neighbor lady'd get their pennies together for a bottle of wine and sit sippin' on the front porch all afternoon." Margy took a long drag on her cigarette.

"It probably looks to you that these kids of mine don't have much, but we're doing a damn sight better for them than my folks did for me. My kids ain't going to go without food like I did. We keep 'em in clothes, too."

I could hardly wait to get home and write my new discovery in my journal. That night I wrote:

April 12, 1988
Margy finally put into words something I've been trying to understand. We all want to give our children a better life than we have had, but each family's experiences place them at a different starting place. It could take generations for some families to progress to the level that is another family's starting place. Still, we're all on the same ladder and have the power to pull each other up, but not in giant leaps—only one rung at a time.

In the sink-or-swim havoc of my first year, with Jenny among my coaches, I was learning to swim. Gradually my fear and discomfort floated away, as I grew to love the parents as much as I loved the children. Spending time with them on their turf eased me through the culture shock and expanded my comfort zone. The gold couch didn't seem so grungy; the dirty children were easier to hug, kiss, and hold because they and their parents were now people to me. I was no longer an outsider watching with no control. The feeling that I was doing something that might make a difference became stronger than my desire to escape.

✂

For the three months Jenny stayed at the shelter, she was in my classroom daily. She was fascinated with the teaching profession and wanted to know how I had learned to teach, how I prepared lessons, how I knew what each child should be learning. We spent hours before and after school talking about my career. She knew my gripes about the education system and that I was committed to changing the status quo. She was also intrigued by how much I liked teaching.

"I want to be a teacher," she said while we were tidying up the room after a crowded day of thirty-plus students. "You actually get paid to do something that you really like to do."

I paused and straightened my aching back. "You should do it. This would be a good job for you. You love kids," I said as I tossed her a book to put on my desk, "you love my teacher's editions, so why don't you go to college and get your teaching certificate? Then you can come back and be my teaching assistant."

"You'll be old and retired by that time," Jenny said with a grin.

"Then you can take over. All this can be yours," I said, laughing as I held my hand out to the desperate-looking classroom.

"And all the kids will love me because we'll only do math one day a week in my class," she said.

"Love isn't everything," I said as I turned off the lights on our way out the door. Then I slid my arm around Jenny's shoulders. "But it's the most important thing."

✂

I often wondered how Jenny had escaped the craziness of her home life with so few visible mental and emotional bruises—although her attitude and outward vitality could have been one way of hiding the turmoil of home. Jenny was the one functioning member of her family, the one real adult. Her stepfather was in prison when she first came to the shelter, which was probably why Jenny and her mother ended up there. Jenny's mother had an intense need to be taken care of by a man, which had led to a cycle of marriage, divorce, and remarriage. Jenny had been sexually abused by at least one of the men in her mother's life, and perhaps more. This had left deep scars of terror, which would surface later in her life in frequent nightmares.

Jenny's mother, though she wasn't an unkind woman at all, seemed incapable of any real effort around the house and insensitive to what was going on around her, so Jenny looked after her younger siblings, as well as a number of nieces and nephews of older siblings who returned on and off to live with them. There was always some sort of crisis. "It's crazy in there," Jenny would tell me while we stood shivering outside of her trailer with our arms wrapped around ourselves against the cold. Sometimes we would stand there talking as long as she could endure the weather before she would go inside. These were the only moments I would see her down, though they never seemed to last long. The family adored her. She was the one person up and doing, meeting their needs, the only one who seemed to have a grip on reality.

At the school, she was free to be her best and happiest self. Each morning as I pulled up at the shelter she would prance gracefully to my car, sometimes stopping to do a pirouette. I always marveled at her contagious smile and the fire in her eyes. Her playground was a glass-infested gravel site, her only privacy a trailer turned into a group bathroom with feces smeared all over the walls, her home more a wreck than a refuge. But she was one of the rare children psychologists call a "Super Child," one who for unknown reasons rises above all of the injustices, ugliness, and damage in her world and moves on. They are kids with a strong will to survive and to be somebody. Where the strength comes from to become a positive product out of the most negative environment no one really knows, but in my work I have seen few children with a history like Jenny's who are as stable as she was. She would not be battered down. I could only imagine what she could be if she were not held back by the environment that surrounded her.

✄

I considered Jenny my friend. She was as indispensable to me during the three months she was at the school as the parents she brought in became. Our personalities were similar, too—neither of us was easily discouraged and we both shared a love for people. Like me she was a "chocoholic," and sometimes after a particularly hard day we would sit down at my desk and indulge ourselves. One day as we munched I joked that I had become a teacher because I didn't have the courage to become an actress.

"The classroom is my stage and I try out all of my techniques on you guys," I said. We both laughed, knowing there was some truth to my story.

"You know, that's my secret dream, too," Jenny said, dramatically flipping her dark hair over her shoulder.

Something clicked inside of me just then. Not long before, I had visited the University of Utah to speak to a graduate class in speech and drama. The professor, Dr. Samuels, ran a special drama course for youth, and his students had given benefit performances for places like the shelter. Dr. Samuels had told me about a program of singing and dialogue that his gifted kids were going to be working on for their summer workshop. The theme was homelessness. I had been asked to visit the troupe later in the month to give them some background and answer questions. And here was Jenny homeless and dreaming of the stage.

I made a phone call to Dr. Samuels gave a strong sales pitch and Jenny was in.

"Bring her with you when you come to talk to these kids," Dr. Samuels told me.

When I speak to groups now, I talk about the causes of homelessness and especially what homelessness does to children—the embarrassment, the setbacks in school, the deprivation of almost everything we take for granted. I try to give some understanding to my audience of what they can do as part of a community and relay the idea that there is hope for change. Ordinarily bubbly and articulate, Jenny sat silently as I spoke to the students in Dr. Samuels's theater group. When I finished, I asked if there were anything she wanted to say, motioning for her to come up and take my spot at the center of the stage.

"It's lonely," Jenny explained at the microphone. "It gets really lonely and there's not anything to do around the shelter. It's easy to get bored." There were few kids her age, especially girls, at the shelter during the time she was there. She talked about how she didn't have much to wear and didn't like to get close to friends for fear they would find out that she lived at the shelter. "One night this other kid and I took a cab to the shelter from downtown. We had to tell the driver to drop us off by the shelter, and it was pretty embarrassing."

There wasn't a sound in the auditorium until Dr. Samuels spoke up and invited Jenny to join the production. She would be the troupe's consultant, their expert on homelessness, as they worked on their piece.

Jenny was elated, frightened, honored. But for the next two weeks, she struggled. She was involved with gifted artists who took their craft very seriously, kids who were talented and used to working hard. This was my first experience with seeing Jenny get really discouraged. She didn't have the physical stamina to keep up with these kids, or the emotional support system required for such tremendous risk-taking. Some days she simply woke up to too much chaos at home to be able to leave and come to rehearsal.

The other kids were very supportive, however. They would perform scenes for her, ask her questions, respect her feedback. She worked with them on writing the show, did some role plays with them, and enjoyed just being a kid with the others during lunch. When the play opened, Jenny performed in a scene and was listed in the program as a creative consultant and volunteer student.

After the performance, Dr. Samuels continued to spend many hours with Jenny, hoping to be the force that would break the cycle of poverty and homelessness in Jenny's life.

Dr. Samuels recognized, as I would come to see, that short-term, one-time efforts didn't fix things. To help make a difference, someone needed to establish a long-term relationship and provide those positive family and educational experiences Jenny had never had and would perhaps never have otherwise. With Jenny, Dr. Samuels wanted to be that someone. He and I made something of a pact to keep tabs on Jenny and in touch with one another to compare notes and see how she was doing.

During the summer, Dr. Samuels called to tell me that he wanted to follow up the theater experience for Jenny with a trip to San Francisco with the troupe to perform at a competition. Taking her on the trip to San Francisco would give her a chance to get out of her rocky home environment for a while. He hadn't told Jenny about his idea, yet. First, he wanted my help in getting permission from Jenny's mother.

"Jenny knows everybody in the troupe. She'll get out and see some places and meet some new people. It will be good for her," he said, and I knew he was right. By this time Jenny's family had moved into an apartment, so I told Dr. Samuels that I would go after school and reassure Jenny's mother that Jenny would be in good hands.

"I'm counting on you, Stace," he said.

As I pulled up at the address, I checked my lipstick and hair in the rearview mirror. I had met Jenny's mother before, and I didn't think she'd care how I looked, but I wanted Jenny on this trip, so I was taking no chances.

I found Jenny's mother rocking in the same chair she had been in every time I'd seen her, sitting in front of the same TV, petting what looked like the same calico cat. The halls of the house were choked with mounds of laundry, half-packed boxes, empty cartons, and the air was bitter with smoke.

"Mrs. Peale, how are you?" I said. Jenny's mother nodded in time with her rocking.

"A little tired today," she said.

"Do you remember me? I'm Jenny's teacher from the shelter." More nods.

"I'm glad you got into a house. It's nice."

"Jenny isn't here," she said.

"That's OK. I came to talk to you. Did Jenny tell you about the play she helped with at the university last spring? Well, the director would like her to go help put the play on again in San Francisco. It won't cost her anything to go, she just needs your permission."

We went the rounds for almost half an hour, agreeing that Dr. Samuels was a nice man and Mrs. Peale a busy woman, before she finally said about Jenny, "She can do what she wants."

Jenny went with the troupe as Dr. Samuels's assistant and loved the attention, the independence, and being part of something important. She also loved the hotel pool, where she spent most of her time rather than attending workshops or classes, Dr. Samuels would inform me later.

"Wait till you see my tan," Jenny said over the phone from the hotel room.

"I'll bet you're gorgeous," I told her.

San Francisco was a blast, according to Jenny, except for all the rules Dr. Samuels had established for the trip. Jenny had lived most of her life without supervision and was frustrated with the restrictions. No one had ever said to Jenny before, I love you, but follow my rules. When I say go to bed at nine o'clock, I mean go to bed at nine o'clock. When I say get off the stage, I mean get off the stage.

"But it wasn't too bad," she admitted. "Most of the time."

✂

Work kept me busy as new kids entered the shelter school each week, and as the months passed, I lost weekly contact with Jenny. Dr. Samuels still saw her regularly, though, and kept me up-to-date. He drove her to school, helped her transfer once or twice, came to Jenny's family's aid financially at times for her sake. He considered it a responsible behavior in Jenny to ask for help when she knew she needed it, and he was serious about being there for her.

Jenny herself called me periodically. She called once to say her birth father had moved back East, and she and a friend had run away to live with him, but they were back—thanks to Dr. Samuels's help. When a newly born niece died, she came to see me in person so we could cry together. All I could do was tell her how sorry I was and offer her an avenue in which to grieve. She was thirteen then, already too serious with boys years older than herself and missing too much school from what Dr. Samuels had told me. I reminded her that I still expected her to come back to be my teaching assistant, and I tried to deny that we were drifting further apart.

After Jenny had run away and come back, knowing things were going no better at home for her, Dr. Samuels invited Jenny to live with his family. He said if Jenny wanted to, he would go to court and they could request that she be placed with him under some sort of foster status; however, as part of the deal, she would need to follow the house rules. She would have a curfew. She would have to go to school every day and do her homework. He made it clear he would only be willing to make the commitment if she would accept the structure.

This was a big chance for Jenny. It could have made all the difference in her life, but she could not accept the rigid expectations. At nearly fourteen, she had never had any sort of structure imposed upon her or any kind of traditional upbringing. Both Dr. Samuels and I tried to convince her that structure was good, but she had nothing to compare it to. To have a dad to come home to at night, to have a piano downstairs she could learn to play, a house in a middle-class neighborhood—she didn't know if these were good things. You can say to someone, "I can offer you this," but how does she know if it will make her life better or not if she's never had it, never even seen it?

Jenny was one of my first lessons with this particular complexity of working with people and deprivation. I came into my profession believing if I could just explain to people how to accomplish a task that was for their benefit, show them a better way, they would be able to see what I was offering was good—to see it my way—and act for themselves. I didn't believe in the quick fix, but I believed fixing things and people was possible—if I could just teach them, share with them what I knew, love them enough.

I learned quickly that just telling someone doesn't work. You literally have to take them by the hand and work at tasks with them. You have to be mentor, boss, cheering section, mother, drill sergeant, whatever it takes—and sometimes this doesn't work, either. I also learned that a few hours, even as intense as I was, could not compensate for the many years Jenny, or any of my students, had gone without. I could help—I could teach, support, and love—and people would change, but they would change themselves. Karen, who had begged my mother to adopt her baby girl, had eventually. She was enrolled in the community college now, and my mother received a letter from her every now and then. Maybe Jenny would do the same.

✂

I called Dr. Samuels when I got home the night Jenny phoned me about the baby.

"I know," he said. "She told me."

"Do you hear from her much?"

"Not regularly," he said. I could hear him settling back into a chair.

"How's she doing? Do you know?"

"I made an appointment for her tomorrow for a prenatal checkup. I've met the father. He's about twenty-one. He's a nice enough guy, says he wants to marry her, but Jenny doesn't want him to just because of the baby."

I remained quiet on the other end of the line.

"She'll do what she wants to, Stace. She's still a good kid."

"I know," I said quietly. "Tell her to call me."

A month or so later, Jenny did call again. "I need to work off some community hours for. . . ," she paused, then spoke, "for a crime I did." It was clear that she didn't want to elaborate so I didn't ask any questions. Instead, I invited her to spend the following day with us on a field trip to a local historical farm.

"It will be fun," I said with as much casualness as I could muster. "It will give you a chance to see one of the great places you can bring your baby to after she's born. And besides that I miss having you around as my teaching assistant."

At the farm, we walked side by side along a path while the children explored. It was late spring, one of the first really warm days of the year. Jenny's beautiful round belly and the glow about her brought back memories of my own first pregnancy. I told her of my experience when I was young, hoping that my own trials would not have been in vain if they would help Jenny. I told her that her fears would be normal and reminded her gently of the responsibility she had now committed to.

"You come second now. The baby's needs are first," I said before realizing suddenly that this was nothing new to her. She had been a caretaker since I had known her; her needs had always come last.

The children responded warmly to Jenny as they always had when she was in the school with me. While she helped pass out lunch sacks, they mobbed around her trying to describe the old machines they had seen and tell her about the horses. She promised the sixth-grade boys that as soon as lunch was finished she would go with them to examine an old steam engine. While we ate, she took my hand and fingered the large, "diamond" ring I was wearing.

"Where'd you get this?" she asked.

"It's my engagement ring. Curtis, one of my third graders,

95

gave it to me last year. He's going to come back and marry me when he's eighteen."

"What does Greg think?"

"It's good for him to know there's a little competition. He's got to treat me right, now." Jenny laughed, the same infectious, bubbly giggle.

"I still want to teach some day," she said, a little wistfully, watching the children eating and roughhousing on the grass. I gave her a squeeze.

"Anything is possible, Jenny, if you want it badly enough," I told her.

"If you did it so can I," she said, smiling with a flash of that confidence I fell in love with when we first met.

✄

A few months later, Jenny gave birth to a beautiful girl, just as I had ten years before. I held her baby in my arms and quietly prayed for both mother and child. Since that time, both Dr. Samuels and I have been waiting in the wings to prompt Jenny from time to time when she needs somebody. She doesn't come by often, but when she does, I talk to her about her baby and her plans. Dr. Samuels always asks if she wants to hear the things she doesn't want to hear. It's not a lecture, just hard questions about where she is and where she wants to be. He sees his role as something of a mechanic: Jenny checks in with him, and he gives her a psychological tune-up. He is still committed to her welfare and her success, still knows that real help is not a one-shot deal.

I still face the frustration in my work of wanting to do more. It would be more accurate to say that I want to dictate more results. I want homes, food, education, and security for my children. I want jobs for their parents. I want Dale to stop drinking; I want JoAnn to not have to be afraid of her husband anymore; and I want Aaron to do his homework. But we can't impose our own goals, wishes, or help on anyone. We can only teach, support, and love. We give them more opportunities, more choices. Then we love them regardless of the choices they make, hoping that they will learn to make better ones in the future.

I want good things for Jenny and so does Dr. Samuels. For now, we'll have to wait; but we'll be there when she wants them badly enough for herself. ⇨

✏ LESSON PLAN ✂

Worry Wok

Materials: A wok, paper, pencils, scissors

Object: To help kids learn to differentiate between kid responsibilities and adult responsibilities. (Underprivileged kids often burden themselves with worries about responsibilities that should be their parents' or situations that they cannot control.)

Activity:

1. Place a large wok on a table.

2. Ask the children to help you come up with a definition of *rights* and *responsibilities*. For example: *Rights* are things we deserve. *Responsibilities* are things we have to do.

3. Brainstorm for ideas on what rights kids should have. For example:

   security   the right to be heard

   education   food   love

4. Continue to brainstorm and create lists of responsibilities pertaining to children and adults. For example:

Responsibilities of kids	Responsibilities of adults
keep our bodies clean	provide security for kids
help tend brothers and sisters	provide food
do homework	pay bills

5. Have the children write down ten worries they have.

Close: Have the children cut any worries from their list which have been identified as grown-up responsibilities or things they cannot change and put them into the wok. Invite each child to read the worry before he or she puts it into the wok.

Help the children see that they are not alone in things they worry about and that many adult responsibilities are beyond their control. Decide with the students to let go of these worries so that they can concentrate on their responsibilities as children. ✂

 Blowin' Sugar

Anne Johnson snuck into the back of the classroom as I passed out an egg carton and a handful of small pom-poms to each student. While I asked the class to put their books away and get ready for math, Anne quietly took a seat behind her own children—Angel, David, and Marcus. This particular arithmetic lesson was aimed at helping the students understand that fractions are merely parts or portions of things. We used egg cartons as apartment buildings, pom-poms as tenants, and worked with concepts such as: If one person is home in a building that has twelve apartments, it means one out of twelve or one-twelfth. Most children don't understand something as abstract as math unless you connect it with something they can already relate to. Apartment buildings and people were a common thread, so we started there.

"Remember the rules," I reminded the class. "Give everyone a chance to find the answer before you call it out." I began with a simple story problem and enjoyed the look of concentration on the children's faces as they worked toward a solution. As understanding clicked for one student after another, the excitement mounted. At the head of the rally was Anne Johnson. She couldn't keep from smiling, anxiously fidgeting as if she had uncovered a magic pebble that had to be kept secret. I grinned, knowing she couldn't hold back much longer.

"Go ahead, Anne. Tell us the answer." "Three-twelfths or one-fourth," she burst out proudly, while her children cheered wildly.

As we ended our lesson, Anne asked, "Is that it? Is that all there is to fractions?"

"That's it," I responded, smiling.

✂

The first time I saw Anne Johnson, I thought to myself, *Wow, this woman could be a movie star or a model.* She was a tall, fine-featured black woman, who smiled shyly as she introduced the three children she guided into the classroom in front of her. When, after a few weeks, she confessed that she had dropped out at a young age and was terrified of school, I invited her to sit in with her children.

"I'm too old to learn nothin'," she said, flashing her infectious, shy smile.

"You might be surprised," I replied, grinning. You couldn't help but smile back at Anne.

"You really think so?"

"Come and see."

I think it was more than just math that Anne started coming for. As we talked after class, I got a glimpse into the tragic life Anne had lived, a life her children seemed destined to inherit. No one had taken the time when she was younger to show any interest in her education, to help her develop her beautiful voice, to offer her little bits of success to build her confidence. Anne had missed the chance to be a child when she was young, and I could see that she was trying desperately to gain some of that childhood back in the classroom now with her children.

Anne was typical of so many of the homeless and others on the streets. When you grow up in poverty, often childhood is stripped from you. Your playgrounds are drug-infested, your nights full of people who don't offer you positive pastimes. Since most constructive leisure and educational activities cost money and you don't have any, you tend to waste a lot of time. If you are raised by people who don't understand effective problem solving or critical thinking, you don't learn the skills you need to make it in this world. No one teaches you to develop your talents, and without encouragement you grow up with wasted potential and little self-esteem. Anne could have been a model or a singer or done any number of positive things with her life, but no one had taught her to recognize her talents or to believe in herself.

If you have grown up with men who beat women, too often you marry a man who beats you. Or someone who hooks you for drug money because you have too little self-worth to say no. Maybe someone who eventually lands in prison or leaves you, or who you are left to run from if you can. Nobody teaches you the dangers of drugs or what alcohol can do to a baby in the womb. Nobody tells you why you should stay in school.

The cycle can be unending. Those who come from generation after generation of people who have never owned land or a home, never earned a high school diploma or had fostered in them a sense of hope for a brighter future, find it nearly impossible to pass these values on to the generations that follow them. When a family doesn't have what it takes to give the kids positive experiences, if an outside source—a church group, the school system, the courts—doesn't step in to help, odds are heavy that the children will continue the pattern.

Little by little I learned of the domestic violence in Anne's family, a tragedy that is one of the chief causes of homelessness among children. I learned of the substance abuse, the heavy dependence on alcohol and drugs, which is too common among this population. I didn't understand the reasons behind the widespread alcohol and drug use among the very poor and the homeless for a long time. Why was I surrounded by parents who loved their children but who destroyed themselves and their families? Why did they buy drugs instead of food? Why didn't treatment programs work? But as the years passed, I saw that when people have so little to look forward to, so much pain to cover up, and so little to lose, it's easy to take the quickest and easiest high. And after living for years on the edge of their world, I couldn't blame them anymore.

This was Anne's story, too. She was the product of generations of hopelessness. Her children were better off than many—they were fed and had clothes, and when Anne was sober, they didn't lack affection. But they had missed a lot of school and a lot of childhood. They had come to rely on each other because they couldn't always count on their parents. They didn't want to lose their mom; they had been in foster care before and knew that they could be taken away from their mother again, so they were careful not to arouse suspicion. But they were tired of playing the role of protector to their mother when she was drunk, tired of being embarrassed and forced to cover for her. And even though Anne Johnson loved her children deeply, that wasn't enough to help them until she could help herself.

✂

Anne had alluded to needing to make some changes in her life, and one day as I was walking down the hall, I overheard her talking with her caseworker about starting in-patient treatment for her chemical dependencies. She was willing, but she was concerned that her children would be sent to different foster families. A judge had warned her that if the state took custody one more time, she might not get them back.

"They're my babies," I heard her cry.

Anne glanced at me as I passed, and I saw the anguish in her eyes. I waited until she was gone, then slipped back down the hall and into her caseworker's office.

"What's up with Anne?" I asked.

"She's finally asking for some help," Shawn explained, closing a file on his desk. "The window's open. She's scheduled to check into the center on Monday."

"What about the kids?" I said.

"We've still got to make some arrangements."

"Who's going to take all three of them? And they're black," I added, knowing we simply didn't have a large black population in Salt Lake City.

"We're working on it," Shawn said. Anne knows she needs help—that's a good start."

For the rest of the day I kept hearing Anne's plea for help, her plea to keep her family intact, her children together. That night I went home and told Greg the tragic story of this beautiful family. Half-joking, I said, "Gosh, I wish I could just bring 'em home and save her all that trauma." My statement started a thought that hung around in the back of my mind through the evening as I helped Greg with dinner and the kids with their homework.

That night I couldn't sleep. Over and over I woke in a panic, thinking of Angel Johnson and her brothers—Marcus, the responsible oldest child, and David, the class clown. David used jokes and laughter to hide his embarrassment at not being able to read. One of his favorite jokes was about Angel's hair, which was about one inch long and very brittle; it never seemed to grow. In a melodramatic voice, he would describe how rats had eaten his sister's hair. Then he would put on this mournful look and pat Angel's head, while she laughed right along with the entire class. They were wonderful kids, all three of them, and they shared a special closeness. They covered for one another and stayed close in class, often standing in a kind of chain, touching, making sure they were always near each other.

As I thought about them, I caught myself wondering, Could I take Anne's children while she was in treatment? Could they just stay here with us? I kept pushing the thoughts aside, trying to go back to sleep, until finally I decided I needed to listen to that tiny voice inside me.

The next morning at breakfast I told Greg how I felt. "We

need to bring them here," I explained quietly. "I just know it."
Greg nodded.

"Let's see if there's a way," he said, and by the time breakfast was over, we had some of the practical details worked
out. Before work that morning, I went to find Shawn, Anne's
caseworker.

When I told him about my plan, Shawn said in a tolerant,
fatherly tone, "Do you understand what you're asking to do?"

"I think so," I said.

"These are kids who have suffered a lot of hard knocks.
Are you prepared to deal with their wounded spirits? Do you
understand the liabilities, the legal end of it?" he pressed me.

"Yes," I said. I understood that my conscience would hold
me liable if I didn't. I knew I just couldn't allow the Johnson
children to be separated again. These three needed each
other, especially now.

Shawn sat me down and gave me a history on the children. They had seen a lot in their young lives. Constant expo-
sure to heavy drug use. A father in prison. It was alleged that
Anne had been beaten so many times by their father that the
children had a terrible fear of men.

"Greg would be a perfect role model for them, then," I
interrupted. "They need to see that not all men solve problems with physical abuse and violence."

"You've also got two kids of your own to think about,"
Shawn reminded me.

"Brandon is always complaining about wanting a brother,"
I said. "Angel would be in Nichole's class at school."

"Stacey, I'm not arguing about it being darn nice or even a
good thing to do . . ." he started.

"Then help me," I pleaded. "And hurry up, before I
change my mind."

Once I got Shawn on my side, the next step was to break
through the red tape and roadblocks in the system.
Sometimes we get caught up in policy and forget that we are

dealing with real people to be healed. On the other hand, the rules are there for a reason. Doing what I was trying to do is generally not a good policy. There are legal questions as to who is responsible for these children. It's disruptive to your home, especially if you have kids of your own. Shawn was right; these were damaged children. You have to have some strong children to understand the dynamics of what's happening, to accept these strangers into their home and private lives. And the shelter likes to help families function as families, not to break them up. This family was going to be separated, though, and this is why I just couldn't let go.

I knew I had to take this family home, and I made up my mind that nothing was going to get in the way, even though I understood the reservations I might have if someone came to me asking to do what I intended doing. I called the social services agency the family was associated with, explained that the mother was starting in-patient treatment on Monday, and said I wanted to take the kids. This was a Thursday.

"I can appreciate your concern," the gentleman I was talking to responded politely, "but that just isn't how we do things." He went on to explain the FBI clearance, the interviews, the paperwork.

"There isn't time," I insisted. "Don't worry, I'll take all responsibility." I told him I'd answer for this, that I had to do it, that I'd been up all night knowing I had to. "Just work it out," I ordered.

He wasn't buffaloed, but as I explained more about the circumstances, he was compassionate.

He called back within an hour and said, "You and your husband need to come in and be fingerprinted and fill out the paperwork. You'll also need to bring the mother in so she can sign the paperwork; then they're yours."

Others who work in foster care and have heard this story cannot believe it all happened so fast. It could probably never work out like this again.

When I told Anne, she was shocked. "You're crazy," she said.

"You're right," I agreed. "Just pack their stuff before I regain my sanity."

✄

On March 13, just one day before David Johnson's twelfth birthday, the three Johnson children stood huddled together in our front doorway. I introduced them to my two children, Nichole and Brandon, and the five of them stood looking at each other, not knowing quite what to make of things. To break the silence, I asked my kids to take the Johnsons to the room we had rushed all weekend to get ready for them. This was all it took to get Brandon started.

"Guess what?! My mom and dad bought you new bunk beds and put the stereo from the front room on your dresser. What kind of music do you like? Come on and see your room!" Brandon loved them before they even got to the bottom of the stairs. I could tell already that my family was not going to be the same after this, that this experience would be one that we would come to cherish; still, we were not prepared for either the joy, the hard work—or the noise—that would come to our family over the next four months. You can't take three children into your home and turn them into middle-class kids that feel security and a sense of self-worth overnight. These were three frightened children who didn't have a whole lot of experience with good feelings, security, or success.

What security they did have came from each other. I knew this from the way they stuck together in school. Most siblings in the same classroom tend to tattle on each other, but the Johnsons were adept at covering for one another's mistakes. I saw this close-knit bond in action again on their first morning at our house. When I went downstairs and stuck my head in the room to wake them, I found all three of them cuddled up body to body on one small twin bed.

"Hey, guys, time to get up," I called. Marcus jumped up, startled and embarrassed.

"Angel was havin' nightmares," David offered, as he rubbed his eyes.

"It's okay," I said. "This must feel safe."

"Yeah," Marcus said.

"Don't worry about it," I assured them. "We can get a refund on the bunk beds. You'd better hurry, or I might eat all your breakfast."

Enrolling Angel and David in my own children's public school, I faced firsthand the barriers to education that homeless families face. There were the same unending questions I had encountered years before with Danny, most without answers. Where are their academic records? Have they had their shots? Why is David only reading on a first-grade level? Have they been tested? In my experience, most schools will tell the parents, "Come back when you can give us more information to help your child." In this case, I knew the law; I politely demanded that they take the children while I scrambled to fill in the blanks.

Marcus was a seventh grader. When we tried to enroll him at Fairview Junior High, which served our area, we were surprised at their chilly reception. "This is an academic school," a counselor explained. "This kid will never survive here."

"We'll be just a minute," I said to Marcus, motioning for him to take a seat while I nodded my head towards the counselor's office.

"You don't tell a parent in front of a child that he won't succeed academically," I said as soon as the counselor closed the door.

"You know what the academic standards are here. I just don't think it would be fair to Marcus."

"This is his neighborhood school," I explained. "This is where he belongs now. If he needs extra help at home, he'll get it. He's had a tough life; why can't we give him a break?"

"I don't know if a break is what he'll get at Fairview. He'll be a pretty nontraditional student."

"You can't say no," I said, smiling sweetly. "It's his neighborhood school."

"No, I can't," the counselor sighed, sitting on the corner of his desk. "I'm only trying to help."

"That's all Marcus needs," I said, reaching for the door, "just a little help."

It was true that Marcus Johnson would be competing with children who had experienced a lifetime of support and security. All we were asking the school to do was attempt to fill in some of the losses Marcus had encountered in his difficult life. For a moment I tried to imagine myself as a homeless mother. Would I have the self-esteem to stand up for my child? Would I chalk it up to another experience with the *haves* and the *have-nots?* What is required is a little bending and leaning to adapt to the needs of a child who hasn't had the same experiences, the same luck, and the same good life that children raised in traditional families have had.

In no time at all, Marcus Johnson became one of the most popular kids in the junior high. He was a kind and grateful person—something which will usually get you off to a good start as a newcomer who needs directions to class and help with his locker. The students were interested in his background, which was so different from theirs. When the school newspaper interviewed him, he was so proud he could hardly wait to get home with the news. The excitement was contagious as we all listened to him telling us about all the girls who asked for his phone number.

"What did you tell them?" Greg asked.

"I'd just smile and say, 'I don't know my phone number,'" he chuckled. Marcus was finally a young man living the life that he should have lived.

Both schools turned out to be incredibly supportive. In fact, one day while the kids were out front, we heard a tremendous screech of brakes. I went to the door to see David's special education teacher and her husband talking to David from the car. "We were driving by and I just thought— well, I wanted my husband to meet David," his teacher explained, as I walked up.

The husband extended his hand, and David proudly shook it while he told David how much he'd heard about him and how lucky his wife felt she was to have him in class. David went on about that short visit all night. He couldn't believe that his teacher would stop at his house and talk to him. These small acts of kindness were just what the Johnson children needed.

The Johnson children made an impact around the neighborhood, too. One day Nichole ran into the house screaming, "Mom, hurry, get out here. There's going to be a fight." I ran out preparing to draw on my arsenal of teaching skills to break up a street brawl, fearing that David or Marcus would be in the middle of it. To my surprise, it was little Angel who was sticking an angry finger in to the face of a well-known neighborhood bully.

"I'll kick your ass if I ever see you touch that kid again, you hear me?" she threatened.

"Yes," whispered the bully.

"Now get outta here." I was speechless, and my own children's mouths hung open. As the bully crept away in shame and the crowd of kids broke up, Angel walked over to a pudgy boy who stood cowering beside a large tree. Lovingly she began caressing his head.

"It's okay Jamie, he's gone. But Jamie, you gotta learn to kick some ass." Jamie was stunned. An angel from heaven had descended to defend him.

Seeing me, Angel turned in my direction. "What should we do with him?" she asked as if Jamie were a stray dog.

"Well, he does have a home," I reminded her. "Why don't we take him there?"

We got in the car, and I asked him where he lived, thinking I might have a talk with his mother.

"Can I come in and talk to your mom?" I asked.

"No, she's at work," he said. "She doesn't care anyway. She told me to not be a sissy and learn to get along with the other kids." I could feel a lump in my throat as I looked at Angel in the rearview mirror, who had her hands folded and her head hung.

"It's okay, Angel will look out for you," I promised. "Won't you, Angel?" She looked up and nodded fiercely. As a black child in a predominantly white environment, she knew what it was like to be on the outside.

Life at home was a mix of hilarity and tension. At our house, we have dinner together around the table as a family. This is where we talk. The first night we had dinner with the Johnsons, David didn't use utensils. We were having spaghetti and we all sat back astonished as we watched him eat with his fingers and lick. He was so hungry that he couldn't hold himself back. The first night no one said anything—we just laughed and let him eat. Later it became clear this was his usual method.

"That's how he always eats," Angel said with a shrug, and I looked over at David, who had food from one ear to another. It was like watching a little monkey eat. Gradually we adopted a tender, teasing style to teach him manners—to put a napkin on his lap, to use his fork, to eat properly so he would have the skills he needed.

Brandon, who was younger and could get away with a lot because of the relationship he had with both of the Johnson boys, would say, "David, you have a fork. This is how you use a fork."

"I don't want to use a fork."

"I'll bet you just don't know how to use a fork," Brandon would say.

"Yes I do, but I can get the food into me faster when I use my hands."

Then we would make a game of "Let's see if you can get all the way through the meal using your fork and not getting food all over you."

Eventually David became so conscious of eating properly that when we had ribs, he tried to use his fork. Greg was the first one to get over his laughter enough to explain. "You aren't going to believe this, David . . ."

Mealtime quickly became a favorite time, always filled with laughter. We ate on the patio, and the neighbors started asking if we were throwing parties every night because it sounded like so much fun.

Greg became fast friends with the Johnson boys, something I had been counting on. Greg loves his own children, and they adore him in turn. School projects, sports, growing pains, bad dreams, he is always there for his kids. Our home is no closer to being perfect than anybody else's. We argue, disagree, struggle sometimes to keep the house clean, but we love being together as a family. My mother has often dropped by to find the whole family piled in the bed watching TV or sprawled on the floor playing cards. I was hoping the Johnson children would fit in easily, and I was counting heavily on Greg to make that happen.

He built their trust by talking to them very gently, by listening, and by being their playmate. It got to where I was never sure when Greg got home from work because David, Marcus, and Brandon would catch him as he got out of his car, and they would end up playing baseball or basketball for 45 minutes before he even made it into the house. He put in the time to build a good relationship, and eventually when there were rules to enforce, they respected Greg enough to obey.

And always there was the laughter. Maybe it was Greg in the supermarket swearing to Marcus that chocolate milk came from brown cows, or all the children chanting "Let's go to Shop-*K-O!*" and getting the giggles, or David excusing himself by whining "Did I do that?" and pulling his pants up to his chest to look like Urkel, the TV character, until Greg cracked up. We had always been a silly family, but we had never laughed like we did with the Johnson children. Many of my students have an uncanny sense of humor, and we do plenty of laughing at the school. To me, laughing in the face of what life has dealt them stands as a tremendous testament to the resiliency of the human spirit.

✂

Laughter could not defuse every tense situation, though. When you almost double the size of your family by combining it with another, especially with three kids coming from a troubled home, you are bound to have some setbacks.

For instance, Brandon and Nichole suddenly had to share their physical space and belongings as we went from a family of four to a family of seven. They had to share phones (and the Johnson kids had phone calls like crazy, from neighborhood kids and school friends, once they learned the number), a TV, a bathroom. Now five kids talked around the dinner table and needed attention and help with homework. We even borrowed Nichole's clothes for Angel sometimes. Nichole had a favorite sweatshirt dress, a white one with black sheep on it, that Angel had been eyeing and wanting to wear. One morning when Nichole had left early for student council and I was getting ready for work, Angel begged to wear the dress. Hurrying to gather my teaching materials, I quickly told her to just put something on.

When Nichole came home that day, she gave me a look that said, "Isn't anything mine?"

"What's the matter, Sweetheart?" I asked, sitting on the corner of the bed. I had forgotten about the dress until she explained. I hugged her and told her I understood the sacrifices she was making. "You're learning what I want you to learn," I told her, though I don't know how much that helped at the time. "You're learning how to give."

We had all the typical squabbles at home. Both Nichole and Angel had strong personalities, and when they both wanted their turn playing Nintendo or talking on the phone, Angel did not deal with the stress very well. When she got mad, the harsh words flew out of her mouth and she stormed outside. She even ran away a couple of times because she thought I was too strict. More than once the neighbors looked out to see Angel flying down the street screaming at me, with me running as fast as I could after her. We had to learn as a family that Angel would come back. The first few times she ran, we panicked, but we came to understand that this is how she dealt with things; running was a skill she learned from her family lifestyle.

Angel was fighting the restrictions that came with having a mother and a father around. It was an unusual thing for all three of the Johnson kids, especially getting used to having rules. In a home with two working parents and a family on the go, there had to be a plan. Cooking had to start at 5:00 P.M. to have everybody fed and things cleaned up in time for ball practice. Homework had to be done before video games. They needed to keep their rooms cleaned up like everybody else had to—and what they thought was a clean bedroom and what I thought were two very different things.

At the same time, the Johnsons were experiencing a new-found freedom, a freedom from the burden of being adults too soon. They found neighborhood friends with houses to go to after school, and they soaked it all up. But when they forgot to call to let us know where they were, the next night they couldn't go out. This caused a lot of trouble and arguments. How dare we take away their newfound freedom, they demanded. Typical "kid problems" were magnified because these kids had never gone through them before.

We found out quickly that none of the Johnson children

dealt well with correction. If I got irritated or said anything negative, they went into a funk for the rest of the day. This is when I learned that it is useless to take away privileges from kids who have nothing—it just doesn't work. They say, "So, what else is new?" Greg and I adopted a system of allowing the children to earn the right to do things at the end of the day if they followed through. Family outings and 7-11 slurpees proved to be effective bribes, too.

What we were asking the children to do was to work within a family unit, to follow family rules and to talk to us. Talking to us was a must. We required that the kids let us know what was on their minds and what they were afraid of. They had to be at our dinner table every night to talk. Each child shared what his or her day was like. Through this process they learned how to communicate, to brainstorm about ways to solve problems, to ask for help. We tried to help them understand that it was okay for them to be children, to say "I don't understand this," or "I'm worried about that," and know that a grown-up would help them resolve the problem.

In time they learned that structure could lead to security. Planning always provided something to do and an idea of what came next. They learned they could count on their stand-in mother and father to stick to commitments—ball games, church work, with a school project—no matter how tired they were. The children came to enjoy the positive results of homework time and the achievement that comes with effort. And they grew to enjoy having others make good choices in their behalf, knowing that their needs as children for security and opportunity were given priority.

I remember more good times than bad from those months, though. More fun than fights.

One night early in the summer, as we sat around the kitchen table talking, Greg asked each of the children, "If you could do anything you wanted in life, what would it be?"

Marcus had a ready answer to that question. "I want to be on a baseball team," he said.

David chimed in, "Me too, I've always wanted to play baseball."

"You too?" Greg kidded Angel. No, she shook her head emphatically. She wanted to dance.

Later that night Nichole and Brandon came to us. "Mom," Brandon said, "let's do that, let's put them on baseball teams." I turned to Nichole, whose whole life had been invaded.

"Angel can take dancing lessons in my dance class," she volunteered. I hugged them both.

"Let's go tell them," I said.

So Marcus and David joined the Holladay Baseball League. Nearly every evening, Greg would go out on the street and throw balls around or pile the kids in the van to head to the batting cages or the park to play baseball. He would bat and pitch to them till it was so dark that you couldn't see the ball come past the plate, all the while calling out encouragement.

Baseball games four nights a week dominated our summer. David, Marcus, Nichole, and Brandon were all on separate teams and all needed support and success. The first time David connected with the ball, the screams from the Bess family could be heard in the next county. The look on his face was a mixture of pride and disbelief.

"I did it," he yelled and, of course, forgot to run.

✀

After about four months had passed, Anne was ready for the children to come back to live with her. She had successfully completed her in-patient treatment, and the children were excited and hopeful about living with their mother again. They were also apprehensive. They had grown used to the structure in our home. They had come to count on breakfast in the morning and lunch at noon. They had had teachers who looked forward to seeing them every day, and they knew that they had a home to come to at night and a substitute mom who would help them do their homework, encourage them to be the best that they could be, fill their tummies with warm meals, and support them in school, dance, baseball, and other endeavors.

The children would all be going to the same middle school in the fall, which would help provide the security to make yet another change in their lives. Upon learning of the family's need, a local church group provided one month's rent for an apartment so the family could get off to a good start. As luck would have it, the apartment was located by a very large hospital which provided Anne with her first job and a sense of security. She worked in the housekeeping division while the kids were in school. The neighbors filled the apartment with beautiful furniture and kitchen utensils, and we spent many hours in August moving the Johnsons in and setting them up.

On their last night at our house, I kissed them as I tucked them into their beds.

"Are you guys excited?" I asked, sitting on the edge of Angel's bed. They were, but I was dying. Tomorrow night they wouldn't be here; this room would be empty. No more hearing around the house the multiplication table rap songs the Johnsons had learned while at the School With No Name. No more David at the dinner table. All week I had been telling myself that I had to let go, now. Greg had reminded me, too, though I knew it wasn't going to be any easier for him.

"Your part's through, Stace," he said.

"I know," I answered, but sitting there on Angel's bed on that last night with just a hint of a breeze through the open window and the three children talking softly in the dark about baseball of all things, I thought it was too much to ask. On that night, giving up these kids seemed like the hardest thing I had ever had to do.

During the first few weeks after the kids left, Greg and I

worried a lot about what kind of impact our home had had on them. Did it help or did it hurt? We had provided them with clothes, baseball mitts, bicycles, and dancing lessons—things their mom would probably never be able to give them again. I comforted myself by believing that the children would remember the good family feelings and long for them when they got ready to make choices for themselves. It eased the worry, but not the loneliness.

One morning one of my colleagues was waiting outside my classroom as I arrived at my door, arms laden with books and papers. "Stacey, can you come to my office for a minute?" I followed Scott to his office, dumped my books on his desk, and waited for him to speak.

He didn't want me to hear about this from another source, he began. "The other night, I was at the grocery store. It's right by the liquor store," he explained quickly, then continued. "I walked out and bumped into the Johnson children. They were dressed in shabby clothing, begging for money. They each had a cup in their hands, and when they saw me they hung their heads. When I asked where their mom was, David pointed to the liquor store. I walked over to talk to her," he finished softly. "She was counting pennies and nickels out to the cashier."

My heart sank. All of the hours Anne had spent in recovery, all of the hope we had for her and the children blown right out the window. I wanted to ask Scott if he were sure, but there was no point.

"You had the kids all summer, didn't you?" Scott said.

I nodded.

"I'm sorry," he said. We were both sorry. He didn't have to say what he might well have said next—that's how it goes. I knew how low the long-term success rates were for programs like the one Anne had participated in. A pall hung over the rest of the day at work, a heaviness so real I felt as though Anne's failure were my own.

After work I shared this story with Greg as we worked in the yard. In the middle of my story we heard two familiar voices yell out to us from the streets.

"Stace, Greg, hi!" Marcus and David were visiting Gus, they cheerfully explained. His mom had picked them up from their new apartment for a visit. I couldn't help but notice how carefree the boys were as they rode the bikes they had gotten while they lived with us. I didn't question them about what I had heard, knowing they would have been embarrassed that I knew they had been panhandling, even if it was for their mother.

Brandon was ecstatic to see his "big brothers." "Come play catch," he demanded. "No one will play catch with me." Soft-hearted David couldn't bear to refuse him.

That night, after Marcus and David returned home, Brandon asked, "Why can't they come back to stay for good? I liked having big brothers again."

✀

We all missed the Johnson children, and it didn't help knowing the direction the family seemed to be headed. For four months my family had loved and sacrificed on behalf of these kids, and you can't imagine how difficult it was to let them leave us. At dinner we missed the rap and the laughter. My kids missed their baseball buddies. It was an adjustment, being a family of four again.

Sometimes when I was lonely for their voices I would turn on my answering machine and reminisce to the rap:

This is the house of Greg and Stacey Bess,
So listen to the rest of this mess.
We're on the microphone 'cause we're not home,
So leave a message at the sound of the tone.

I remember the seven of us lying on the bed in the master bedroom, giggling as we attempted to record the answering machine message. When the boys began, "This is the house of Greg and Stacey Bess," the girls threw themselves on the bed in laughter. We'd had to stop and start over too many times to count. Finally, Greg came up with a plan. "Nobody look at anybody," he ordered. We closed our eyes and tried to ignore the others as they concentrated on their part. When we had finally finished recording the message, we fell apart in hysterics.

The next day the children all sat on my bed to listen to the messages. The digital box indicated six calls. Angel pushed the button, and we listened eagerly. Each message began with a moment of complete silence, followed by out-of-control laughter.

This laughter and warmth extended into the lives of my own adult family members. I had overlooked what the children should do if they needed help at school, assuming perhaps that they would call me at the shelter. One day, when David was feeling sick at school he called not me, but my husband's mother.

"Hi Grandma, this is David." There was a long pause while she tried to recall if she had a grandchild named David. "Grandma, I'm sick, please come and get me." At last a light went on and she realized that this was one of the little children living in our home.

"David, honey, you caught me off guard," she said. "I'll be right there."

On another day my sister Stephanie and Mike, a boy she had been dating, had come over to visit. They were lying quietly with the kids on the trampoline, soaking up the sunshine, when out of the blue, Angel teased, "Blowin' sugar, Stephanie?"

"Doin' *what*?" Stephanie giggled.

"Blowin' sugar, you know," she looked down to where Mike was holding Stephanie's hand. "Holdin' hands with your boyfriend. Where I come from, that's blowin' sugar."

For years to come, whenever we saw couples snuggle or kiss, someone in the family was certain to sing out Angel's phrase, "Hey, blowin' sugar?"

✂

Greg and I picked up the kids to come visit regularly over the next few months, and we dropped by the apartment with goodies and to see how the Johnsons were getting on. I knew Anne wasn't completely clean and sober, but the family seemed to be doing all right. That is, until I knocked at the Johnson's apartment around the middle of December to deliver Christmas gifts. I was met with a pile of abandoned newspapers and flyers in front of the door. Through the window I could see nothing but an empty room.

"Can I help you?" a woman's voice called out from the next window.

"Where is the family who lives here?" I asked. The woman next door stepped outside and wrapped her sweater tight against herself in the cold.

"They left in the middle of the night. I got so tired of hearing her hurt those kids, I threatened to call the police if she didn't stop," she told me.

"Damn," I said to myself. "Where have I been?" The neighbor woman, seeing my consternation and my arms full of gifts, invited me in. She offered me a cup of tea and asked how I knew the family. Then she told me what she had seen of the Johnsons.

"She pushed those boys out the door into the rain and said, 'You just hurry it up,'" the woman told me as I took comfort in the hot tea. "The boys were crying as they ran down First South. They came back soaking wet some time later. I looked out the door and saw them hiding something under their shirts but couldn't see what.

"The next day when their mom went out to the liquor store I knocked on their door to see how the kids were. The table was covered with piles of cigarette butts. I asked them if they'd gone out the night before to get the butts, and I could tell they were ashamed. 'Don't tell Momma we told you,' they said. 'She'd whop our behinds bad.'"

I learned that many nights Anne woke her children, shaking a broom at them and yelling, "I need a smoke. Get up to the hospital and gather up all the cigarette butts from the ashtrays."

Why hadn't the kids told me about this problem, I wondered out loud. I remembered numerous hints and innuendoes that, in hindsight, suddenly made sense. Occasionally, when I had stopped by to visit, one of the children might say, "I'm tired. Mama was drinking last night and she made us get up." But they would always stop right there and I hadn't questioned them further. I knew she wanted company when she got drunk, and it didn't matter what hour. Still, I never felt fear for them. Anne could be a little harsh, but I knew that she loved her kids passionately.

I realized then that I didn't know what kind of a mother Anne was at home. From the sound of things, she was repeating her own childhood experiences. I wondered where all the good people were while Anne was growing up. Is it possible that throughout Anne's whole life there wasn't one person willing to teach Anne to love herself? Is it possible to expect any change to take place if we don't take the time to love?

✄

A few months after Anne's family disappeared, we received a phone call.

"It's Marcus," a voice that sounded far away said. "Can you send me my baseball mitt?" He had left it at the house.

"Marcus," I said, fighting back the flow of tears, "where are you? I've missed you guys so much."

He was silent, then I could hear him ask if it would be all right to tell Stacey where they were. A woman's voice in the background said yes. "We're in a foster home," he said. "But we're all together. And we're OK here."

After I spoke to Marcus, I talked briefly to Angel and to David. "I love you," I told each one, "and I hope your new home is happy." I was having real problems talking while I tried to hold back the anguish inside.

"What are Brandon and Nichole doing?" Marcus wanted to know. I was about to send Greg to wake the kids when I realized how late it was. Marcus was calling from a different time zone.

"The kids are asleep. Call in the morning so you can talk to them then," I told Marcus. "Promise me you'll call." I really wanted to go wake up the kids, but it *was* late and I told myself they could talk in the morning. I didn't think to get the phone number, and once we had got talking, we had forgotten all about an address so I could send the mitt.

There was no call the next morning, or the next. My children were furious with me for not waking them and furious with Marcus for not calling back. Brandon was especially hurt. He missed his "older brothers" who had never been too busy to play basketball and baseball with him. They were cool, and he was into cool. Marcus, David, and Angel brought a lot of laughter and a lot of love into all our lives—love they gave and love they led us to give. It's all the same.

We missed them when they left. We still do. ✏

Anger

I am anger;

Black, grey, and red mist.

I make it rain, I make it pour.

I fill up emptiness with madness.

The clouds darken, emotion after

Emotion, I always come back.

Thunder and lightning like

Clashing cymbals. Big booming

Firecrackers. No moon, Bloody Mary.

Black roses intimidate you.

A lone screeching violin.

Nothingness.

—Sixth-grade student

✂

Where Is My Mom?

You've never "seen it all" with a job like this. You wish you had sometimes.

I pulled up just before nine o'clock one February morning and the head social worker cornered me in the parking lot.

"We had an incident yesterday after school that alarmed me," she said with a look of real concern. "The children came across a dead body in the field across from the shelter. Instead of reporting it to the authorities, they threw rocks at the dead man, then looted his pockets." We looked at each other without saying more, but what troubled us most was that the children handled a dead body without the least concern about the blood on their hands that could transmit serious diseases.

"Please talk with your students about it," she said, leaving the lesson plan for Dead Bodies 101 up to me. I headed to class wondering how in the world to turn this eerie incident into a teaching moment. Never in a lifetime would I have believed that I would be dealing with the proper handling of corpses as part of an elementary education curriculum.

A teaching assistant had put the children to work writing in their journals while I was out talking with the head social worker. The topic, written in bold letters on the chalkboard, was THESE ARE THE QUALITIES I HAVE NOW . . . THIS IS WHAT I HOPE TO ACHIEVE . . .

The children didn't even look up as I entered. Knowing that they would eventually have a need to mention the dead man, I patiently waited for them to assess where they were that day and where they would like to see themselves in the future. After a few moments of quiet, though, I couldn't hold back anymore.

"Anything you would like to discuss today," I began, "like finding a dead body in the field?" That put an end to quiet time, especially among my sixth-grade boys.

"Where?" Jason wanted to know. "What field?"

"Come on," I said, and the protests started.

"We didn't do nothin'."

"We just wanted to look."

"If you could see what a dead body looked like and your friends knew where one was, wouldn't you want to go and see?" Ricki said with a look of adventure in his eyes. Jason was leaning back in his chair, his tongue stuck halfway out while he eyed me, waiting to pounce on my response.

"Yeah, I guess I'd be curious, too. I might not have handled things quite like you guys did, though," I told them. I didn't bother with any speeches about touching a dead body being plain gross; instead we spent the better part of the morning discussing reverence to the dead, respecting other peoples' property even if they are dead, and the most important issue of all, "What should you do if you find a dead body that has blood coming from its mouth?" Certainly not touch the body. I was pretty comfortable with the outcome of the discussion until I concluded with my last words of advice.

"If you ever find yourselves in this situation again, call the police."

"Right," Ricki smirked. "Cops don't give a shit. This guy was just another drunk bum."

Another topic for another day.

✄

I realized once again that I hadn't seen it all when Tucker and his mother came to us in another February. We had springlike weather forecast for the next few days, almost as if Mother Nature knew that the children of the streets desperately needed the sun's healing rays. Our Monday at school began with Chrissy taking her turn at the huge map of the United States that hung just opposite our door. The little kids were fidgeting in their chairs or lounging on the floor, and I was holding five-year-old Aimee in my lap while she ran her fingers through my hair and sucked her thumb. Weekends are long for the children, with nothing to do but hang around the halls of the family shelter or out on the dangerous west-side streets. I was always glad to be back together in school where it was safe for them to be kids for a while.

Chrissy was telling the story of her trip to the shelter, tracing her path with yarn and thumbtacks on the big map, adding to a multicolored spiderweb of string and pins. Across the top of the map it read "The Places I've Been." As Chrissy finished, the classroom door banged open, ending all my hopes for a day without incident. The entire class turned at the sound. From where I sat on the floor, the scene I found myself staring at was all the more intimidating. Upon finding the courage to stand up and introduce myself, I slowly reached my hand out to the woman who filled the doorway.

"Hi," I said, "I'm Stacey. How can I help you?" The woman at the door stood over six feet tall and probably weighed more than three hundred pounds. Her thin, jet black hair was pulled straight back, accenting a face that was stern and severe, while her tank top showed off the rough tattoos scrawled across her chest and down her beefy arms. I caught myself staring at the 666s etched in blue around her puffy fin-gers and on the backs of her hands. To my left across the room, my teaching assistant, Lori, stood wide-eyed. This was the kind of woman you got out of the way for.

I would have motioned Lori towards the phone in case we had to call for help, if the woman hadn't been holding a child. Her whole physique seemed incongruous with the tender way she cradled the frightened boy against her body with his face buried tightly in the crook of her neck. When the child turned to look at me, I saw that his eyes seemed to fill the upper quarter of his chubby face. Beneath the spectacular brown eyes were puffy cheeks glazed a cherry red. He was an enormous child, yet as fragile and timid as a butterfly, and he looked to be eight or nine years old. His voice was a whimper.

"Please, Mommy, please don't leave me," he pleaded over and over again.

Sensing that with this interruption more change was coming, the young ones in the classroom edged closer to my side. Little Aimee nudged me, her own eyes wide behind her mop of curly blond hair.

"Aimee needs up," she commanded.

"OK," I said and picked her up for a snuggle. I held her to myself firmly, while she dragged her wet thumb up the side of my cheek. Curiosity got the best of Tonya, a nosy seven-year-old.

"You're really *big,*" she blurted out to the new boy. "How old are you?"

In a thundering voice the woman announced, "This is Tucker. He's five. That's old enough for kindergarten, isn't it?" Startled by her tone and still dumbfounded by her size, I'm sure I didn't make a very good impression as far as my skills as a teacher went.

"Are you his mother?" I managed to get out. Of course she was. Trying to regain some composure, I sat Aimee down and attempted to help Tucker feel at ease about starting kindergarten. While I whispered to him that everything would be OK, his forehead furrowed, and I noticed an unusual look in his eyes, though not the frightened or defiant look I saw in the eyes of the other children who showed up in the doorway. I didn't know what it was.

"Tucker," I said, "this is a fun place to be. We eat snacks, read under our desks, and play silly games." He held my gaze as his mother lowered him to the floor, where he wouldn't stand on his feet. As I knelt down to reassure him, Tucker's chubby hands reached out to push me away.

Shaking, Tucker looked into my eyes and said, "I'm going to kill you."

He turned and grabbed for his mother's arms while I rocked back on my heels. I had never had a child look into my eyes that way and threaten me with such anger. He glared down at me from where his mother held him, and my flesh went cold. Fortunately, the chaos of the classroom didn't give me long to think about it. Tucker soon left with his mother, who assured me that he would be back for school the next morning.

The next day, Tucker and his mother returned, and we began the heartbreaking routine that would repeat itself for weeks. Day after day Tucker would arrive showing no animation or emotion. Holding him gently against her body, his mother would caress him, trying to soothe away his fear. Tucker, sensing that she was going to leave, would bury his face in the crook of her neck and begin to whimper and plead. The scene always ended with Tucker kicking and screaming for her not to leave him. After she left, Tucker would crouch by the door, staring warily at the other children, as if he were afraid they would hurt him. Despite his reluctance to join them, the kids in the class scrambled to put him at ease. Little Aimee stretched up to hold his hand with her slobbery thumb. Her older sister, Jessie, stepped forward to hand him the soft, blue quilt that she had been given when she first arrived at the shelter.

"It's really scary to be new, Tucker," Jessie said, "but you'll like our school. It's fun and Stacey don't treat you mean." I had to smile. Five weeks ago, Jessie had been the terrified one. She cried most of her first day—and so did her mom, just outside the door. Now she was extending the welcome. In the shelter school the kids are all feeling the same topsy-turvy swell of emotions. They are all experiencing homelessness, and somehow this gives them a built-in empathy for each other. The kids who have been in the class a while go out of their way to make new arrivals feel welcome, immediately explaining the point system we use to reward work, the rules of the class, the ins and outs of living at the shelter.

Tucker, however, would not be reached, and for one of the few times in my career, neither I nor my students could console a troubled child. His terror frightened me. Watching him kick, scream, and beg to see his mom ate away at my heart and my nerves. In order to allow the other children some peace and quiet, Tucker and I would leave every half hour or so to say hello to his mother, with me hoping desperately that Tucker would develop some sense of security. With time and the building of trust, most of my students begin to establish a sense of well-being and the knowledge that their parents won't abandon them while they are in school. Not Tucker. Things only got worse.

To keep Tucker in class, I had to keep the door locked. The school was on the second floor of the shelter at the time, only one set of alarmed doors away from the men's dormitory, and I didn't want Tucker running around loose. In addition to the kicking and screaming, he frequently urinated on the floor. I didn't know if this was a way of forcing me to take him to his mother or just something he had no control over. I knew such behavior could also be a sign of abuse, physical or sexual, though I had no evidence of either.

Tucker's mother, Patty, would not consider that perhaps it was too soon to separate the child from her. When I suggested that maybe waiting a year could save him a lot of trauma, she insisted Tucker would adapt.

"He stays with you and that's that," she said. As she towered over me with Tucker cuddled in her arms, still in her tank top despite the cold weather, I felt powerless to argue.

I needed answers to help Tucker, but information about the family was very guarded, and fear kept me from an outright confrontation with Patty. I hadn't been afraid of too many people once I had gotten used to the environment around the school, but I was afraid of her. Meanwhile, I scoured my brain nightly for ways to approach Tucker. Nothing was working. I couldn't get him to leave the corner of the room closest to the door. I felt horrible locking him in, but I didn't want him getting out and ending up lost or hurt. I already couldn't get him off my mind; I didn't want him on my conscience as well.

Finally, I couldn't take any more. One morning I asked Lori to take over the English lesson. Slowly, I sat on the floor next to Tucker and leaned my body against the wall. In the front of the room, Lori pointed to pictures representing the long vowel sounds, and the younger children shouted out, "Eeee. Bee. Eeee," with gusto.

I moved my head close to Tucker's and whispered to him, "Tucker, would you feel safer if I held you in my arms right here by the door?" To my surprise he looked up with eager eyes and climbed into my arms. He was as large as a child twice his age, and it was a struggle to lift him to my chest. Despite the discomfort, I rocked him in my arms until my hands went numb.

When Lori saw that I was tiring, she came over to trade me places. A freshman from college who volunteered mornings three days a week at the school, Lori wore long muslin skirts and what the kids called "Jesus sandals"; she was a child of the sixties born too late. The kids adored her, and from the time she arrived, she rarely went a moment without a child hanging on her or in her arms.

In a monotone cry, Tucker pleaded for her not to touch him. Lori backed off, stunned, and I shifted positions to allow for better circulation in my hands. The class went on with English and then math. Eventually, Tucker fell asleep and I was able to roll him carefully onto his borrowed blue blanket.

Rocking Tucker became a daily activity. It allowed him some peace and gave both of us an opportunity to build trust. As he learned that my kind of touch would not hurt him, that it was similar to his mother's, his entrances to the classroom became less and less dramatic. Slowly I introduced him to the other children by bringing his blanket closer and closer to the learning space. Occasionally, he would sit with me on the floor with a book and let me read to him and ask him questions. Sometimes he would answer by nodding or pointing.

Lori also pointed out one day that Tucker seemed to enjoy music. Whenever the piano would start up, his big eyes would grow even bigger, and he would begin to bounce around. Lori and I began to do musical activities any time we could, just to see him happy. I would watch him from where I stood at the back of the room, puzzled and saddened by his strangeness. He never sang a word, but he would hum. Perhaps he just wanted to feel, and thinking through the words would have ruined the feeling. Whatever the case, I think the music was healing.

After several weeks passed, Tucker's mom started seeing some positive things happen for her. Patty had been looking for full-time employment and had finally found someone who was willing to take a chance on her. This was good news but would set Tucker back in his budding sense of security, since he would not be able to see his mother during school time every day. We tried to convince Tucker that his mother would always come back for him, and we collected fresh clothes and kept them in the school so that we could take care of him in his mother's absence. But part of the process of building trust had been the power he had knowing Mom was in the building. If he wanted to see her, we would go for a visit. With her out of the building at work, all the power was gone; the only person there for him was his stepfather.

Tucker's stepfather always struck me as a dangerous man, and I don't think most people at the shelter felt any different. Shorter than Patty by half a foot, he sported thick glasses and wore his hair cut short. He walked with a slight limp, yet carried himself with a cold authority. His behavior around the shelter was strange and erratic. He had an eerie habit of casting spells on people who walked past him, and he might be the only father figure of one of my students whom I have wanted absolutely no contact with. He frightened me, as he did almost everyone. That was his objective.

"Do not take Tucker to see William," Patty instructed me before she started her job. Tucker's stepfather needed to sleep, she said, but I knew better. I was sure that this guy was at least part of the cause for Tucker's emotional state.

Though things with Tucker took a step backward when Patty started work, I was still feeling comfortable with the progress we had made, and I decided it was time to work on some basic skills with Tucker. Step number one was to give Tucker a pencil and his own notebook. At first he appeared happy with his new possessions.

"Mine?" he questioned with eager eyes.

"Yours," I smiled back. "You can write anything you want to." Taking new hope from Tucker's warm response, I began to teach him the proper way to hold his pencil. I wrapped my right arm around his back and took hold of his hand, so that together we could hold his fingers in the right place. As I applied pressure against his fingers to make the lead appear on the paper, his little body began to tremble.

"Put down that object," he commanded in a deep, rigid tone that startled me.

"The pencil won't hurt you, Tucker," I reassured him, starting to panic myself as he became more and more distraught. While the other children stared, Tucker let go of the pencil and sank to the floor, chanting, "I must not hold that object."

No one laughed or even moved until one of the younger girls started to cry. Lori scooped her up, while we continued to watch. I felt the cold chill again I had felt when Tucker threatened to kill me. Within a few moments, Tucker climbed back into his chair as if nothing had happened. Trembling, I offered Tucker his pencil again and let him experiment with it on his own.

Later that week, the door had been left unlocked, and after turning my back to help another new, frightened child, I found that Tucker was gone. After racing through the building to find him, I panicked and requested the help of the shelter staff. After several minutes of scouring the building inside and out, I decided to make one last search of the second floor. Upon hearing a familiar voice from a classroom, I poked my head in. To my surprise, there was Tucker talking with Wayne, an adult education teacher at the shelter. I stared at the two chatting comfortably together—I had never had the luxury of such a calm conversation with Tucker.

Wayne had a habit of dropping by the school in the mornings on his way to his own classroom down the hall. He would say hi to the kids and ask them what they were doing. Tucker was usually on the floor acting uninterested when Wayne dropped by, but perhaps he recognized Wayne as the man who visited the school and cared about the kids. As I listened to Wayne's gentle voice while he quietly asked Tucker a question, I wondered how many negative male role models Tucker had been exposed to. Relieved that Tucker was safe, I snuck into the room, hoping not to interrupt. A staff member with a mop came in behind me. Wayne caught his eye and pointed to a puddle of urine in the middle of the floor. Then he turned to me.

"Can I talk to you alone?" Wayne asked with a perplexed look. Hastily, he guided me into the hall. "This is a strange child we're dealing with," he said, half smiling and half sad. Nodding, I agreed.

"How did you two get together?" I asked.

"Well," Wayne started to chuckle, "I was teaching my class when this fountain arched up through the crack of my door and fell just short of where I was standing."

"Did you ask him why he chose to do that?"

"Yes," Wayne said, but this time he didn't smile. "When I asked him why he peed through the crack in my door, he said, 'When you lock the door, I can't hold it.' He was shaking all over like he was afraid."

"Any ideas?" I asked. Wayne stood looking at Tucker through the half open door. I saw reflected in Wayne's eyes my own fears of what traumatic incidents in Tucker's past might have produced such behavior.

Wayne shook his head sadly then turned to me. "Just watch him close."

One afternoon, pushed to my limits by emotional exhaustion, I finally worked up the courage to confront Tucker's mother. I saw her peeking in on Tucker through the window on her way in from work, and I made a beeline for the door before I lost my nerve. I caught up to her in a back hallway on the top floor of the shelter.

"Patty," I hollered, and she turned as she heard her name. Facing her, I felt my resolve begin to waver. The hall had no lights or windows, and there was always a haze from the smoke that seeped under the double doors from the single men's lounge. Patty loomed in front of me as frightening as ever, but she looked haggard around the eyes, tired.

"Can I talk to you a minute?" I asked carefully. "It's about Tucker."

Patty eased herself onto the tile floor and leaned against the wall. I stood, wondering what to do next, until she patted the floor next to her.

"Take a load off," she said. "I'm too pooped to stand up any more." I settled down on the cold floor next to her, where the cigarette fumes were heavier. I could feel them burning my throat and eyes. I was barely bigger than some of my students, and I felt like a midget next to Patty.

"What is Tucker so scared of?" I ventured. Patty startled

me by letting out a heavy sigh. Then she stretched her legs out straight in front of her and began describing some of the shaping events of Tucker's young life. She blamed Tucker's fear of being separated from her on numerous run-ins they had had with Child Protective Services in several states. It was simply a ploy, Patty told me, a cover-up for the real reason the state was trying to take her son from her.

"You see, Stacey," she began in her powerful, gravelly voice, "I am a priestess, and Tucker is a guardian in the Satanic church. That's why they were trying to get Tucker away from me, because we belong to Satan's church."

Shocked, despite myself, I blurted out, "Why?"

"To you," she replied with some disdain, "God is your father. To me, my father is Satan. We love Satan like you love God. I call him father because I know he loves me. When I preach about his message he wraps me in a blanket of love, letting me know he is pleased."

I found myself fascinated by the matter-of-fact way she described her love for Satan as we sat side by side in that dark hallway. Her revelation stirred up a whirlwind of emotions inside me. Greatest of all was an ache as she described her need to be loved and accepted.

"You know, Stacey," she sighed, "I feel so much acceptance and love from the members of my coven and my church."

What I found in Patty as we talked was a true "wannabe," someone looking for the bizarre in order to capture attention. Her people gave her acceptance and her religion gave her power—the power to get people to look at her when she talked to them and told them she was a priestess in Satan's church. She certainly got my attention.

I couldn't blame Satanism alone for Tucker's problems, although research I did later indicated that Satanic practices often attract personalities that aren't stable. I was surprised to find that many who are attracted to Satanism come from staunch religious homes. Patty followed this pattern. After being taught that if she were good, God would bless her, when trouble followed trouble, she wondered why God had failed her. She became so discouraged that God had not lightened her load that when Tucker's stepfather came along with a belief that offered power and acceptance, it was not hard to seek out the opposite of the God who had been taught to her all of her life.

To be fair, I do not know what burdens Tucker's stepfather might have carried as a child. I do know that Patty lived a life of emotional trauma and torment, which helped me understand some of her choices.

At six years old, Patty was suffering from a condition that caused her to be the size of a twelve-year-old. The humiliation she felt daily we might never understand—the taunting, the name-calling, the physical and emotional abuse. My heart was torn in two as I listened to her describe her loneliness and the torment she had suffered from her peers. A day didn't go by when she wasn't teased and mocked about her size.

"I never had a friend," Patty confessed somberly, as a tear trickled down her cheek.

✂

After our talk, I often spotted Patty peeking through the small window of my classroom door on her way home from work. If Tucker caught a glimpse of her from his seat, he would leap to the door like a hungry leopard. Apologetically, she would open the door and tell her son to sit down. When this happened, I always tried to take a minute to sit with her and Tucker in the hall and chat. The social workers and I repeatedly offered to set up counseling sessions for both mother and child, but Patty always declined. I put some hard questions to Patty myself when we talked. Do you want this legacy for your child? Do you want him always afraid? When Patty broke down one afternoon and cried, I knew that the monster she presented to the world was a shield against that world, and inside was a tender, damaged person, like her son.

Meanwhile, progress with Tucker was slow. He refused to do almost any assignment, and though he was sitting on a chair at a table most of the time now, there were days when he would revert to his old behavior, crouching by the door, waiting to be rocked. During art, Tucker had a particularly disturbing need to take scissors and cut the arms, legs, and heads off every person he drew. From his determination and intensity, he appeared to get great satisfaction from each careful snip. Lori and I took it in stride, pleased at any participation on Tucker's part.

He did warm up a little to Lori, and he found one more "friend" in an older gentleman from the men's shelter named Steve. Steve was an artist I hired to come in before school to clean my room and make fun art things for me to show the kids. Toward the very end of his stay, Tucker started coming to the classroom at seven in the morning and bugging Steve.

"That damn Tucker," Steve would tell me later in the day. "I don't want him in here."

"Steve," I told him, "you don't know his stepfather. He needs some normal dad experiences. You can give him a few of those." Steve let it go on for my sake, as part of my crusade to see this child healed as much as we could before he left us.

We basically broke every rule to help Tucker by doing this. The children were not supposed to come in until nine o'clock, but we let Tucker come in as early as he wanted, to talk and draw, because we didn't want him left alone with his stepfather. We had no reports of abuse by him, but up to this point, our concerns and suspicions seemed justified by the man's bizarre behavior and Patty's concern for Tucker. Then came a morning in early April.

Around 11:00 Tucker pleaded with Lori to let him use the rest room. This had become a new scheme of his to try to get out and see his mother, though she was actually at work.

This time, though, he had just finished a can of soda, so I had to believe his claim to need to visit the toilet. I couldn't watch the child urinate on the floor and suffer the subsequent humiliation one more time.

Lori was given specific instructions to hold Tucker's hand all the way to the men's bathroom and to stand outside the door. When he had finished, she was to take his hand and return. Tucker was very pleasant that particular day. He went in happily and told Lori he would hurry. After a few minutes, Tucker reappeared with his stepfather, who gripped the back of Tucker's shirt in his fist as he coldly shoved Tucker towards the family's living quarters. Lori quickly explained that Tucker had just been using the bathroom and that he was having a terrific day.

Tucker's stepfather threw a screaming and shaking Tucker into the family's room. Lori ran for help. Soon a staff member was sternly commanding this man to open the door while a crowd gathered in the hallway. When the door opened at last, Tucker stumbled out and scrambled across the hall. Visibly shaken, he lay against the wall and jerked his head back and forth as though he were trying to clear his mind as he spoke.

"I'm scared. Where am I? Where's my mom?" he sobbed. Tucker's stepfather stood in the doorway with a white cloth over his hand as though it had somehow been used to punish the child. I had no question now that this was the person responsible for much of the nightmare this child was living. Tucker was being raised by a dangerous man.

✄

I never was able to learn what happened between Tucker and his stepfather in the room that day. Whatever it was, it warranted Tucker's being taken into protective custody and his stepfather's being ordered to leave the shelter. Two days later, I was surprised to see Tucker with both his mother and stepfather together again on the street. The law had done what it could, but the situation left me alarmed and worried for Tucker's safety. Fortunately, after Tucker left the state a short time later, he was helped by other educators and people who cared. When Child Protective Services looked into the case and found Tucker had something of a record with them, that state took custody and provided him with the security of a hospital, where he can rebuild and heal what others damaged.

✀

The story doesn't end here. A year or two went by, and Patty returned to the shelter. She cornered me and barked out, "You don't remember me, do you?"

Who could forget.

"Where have you been, Patty?" I shot right back. "How's Tucker?"

"The state's still got him in that hospital."

"Is he doing OK?" I said, setting my bag down and moving out of the middle of the hallway so we could talk.

"They say he is. I'm not with William anymore."

I nodded.

"How are you?" she demanded.

"Overworked," I responded.

"Well, I've got a cure for that."

"What's that?" I asked.

"Dying."

"That sounds a little drastic."

"Never fails. Works every time."

Something in the way she talked to me said she was talking about herself.

"Are you OK, Patty?" I ventured. She was thinner, now that I looked closely at her. The flesh hung loosely around what used to be her tight, hawkish face. She wore a knit hat, and the strands of hair hanging out from under it looked wispy and gray. Patty looked old, as I thought about it. Old even for living as hard as she did.

"I been in the hospital. But I'm through with that."

"What for?" I was late, I knew, but this seemed important.

Cancer is what she finally told me. She said she had finished her treatments, but I found out later that the treatments were over only because there was nothing more the doctors could do. Patty had come home, to the shelter and the streets, to die.

As the spring wore on toward summer, Patty and I found a strange love with each other. She needed a friend, and I needed to better understand some things that had happened with her and her child. I started going out of my way to look for her on the sidewalks around the shelter. I would bring food out for her, then sit and talk. We discussed openly her life with Tucker and the Satanic church, and while she used to deride my own belief in God, she was mellowed now and more tolerant.

One day I asked if I could take her someplace where we could talk and be a little more comfortable than the sidewalk. We ended up at a nearby coffee shop, where we talked for hours. That's when I really learned that nobody in her life had reached out with caring and acceptance to call her friend, and she gave me an idea of the horrible unkindness and name-calling she grew up with. At that moment, my heart broke. I wondered what kind of friend I would have been if I had gone to the same schools Patty did. I didn't think I would have participated in the unkindness, but I quietly chastised myself for the conviction that I would have been silent while the torment went on. Like most kids, I would have lacked the courage to say anything or come to her defense.

We laughed a lot on that occasion, too. When Patty's false teeth came out with the pizza she was eating, I couldn't help myself. I held my napkin to my mouth, but there was no hiding it.

"I don't make a very good date, do I?" Patty said.

"You're great," I said, smiling.

"You're the only one who'll stop and visit," Patty admitted. "I been lonely. It was a good thing I run into you." I agreed. It was good for me, too.

Patty started going downhill quickly not long after that. She was still sleeping on the sidewalk while the shelter was full, and the days would go from cold to hot. When I could, after school, I would bring her a blanket and go sit on the sidewalk outside the shelter by the wall to just be there with her. She would blank out for a while and then wake up.

"You're still here?" she'd say. I'd say yes and either help her wrap in a blanket or talk her into moving out of the hot sun. While she was asleep, I sat back against the wall watching life go by on the streets and thinking back on our experience at the restaurant. I had gone home that night and lectured my children about how much harm we can do by standing by and doing nothing. We had been warned at the shelter to stay away from Patty when she was there before, and she didn't invite people to reach out to her with her terrifying presence. None of that seemed to matter now.

Patty was dying on the sidewalk. There wasn't an open spot at the shelter, and she certainly couldn't afford to go back to the hospital or into a rest home. She did have a sweet social worker who would take her into the shelter to get her cleaned up, who saw to it that Patty could maintain some bit of dignity. In her final days, somebody from the medical staff was able to get her into a nursing home. The last time I spoke with her, she said, "When I go, I'll know I had a friend."

Patty had two or three friends in the final months of her life, once her need became so transparent or because she put up less of a fight. And I wept to think, "What if some of them had come when she was younger?" She might not have abused her body the way she did. She might not have helped pass on the legacy she did to her son. She might have given more to the world, who knows?

It's an odd thing, but I still pray for Patty sometimes. I ask God if he can't make up for some of the sorrow she must have felt on this earth. I think sometimes how I might have never known her, how much I would not have learned, how my life would have been less rich. ☞

Hungry Eyes

It was the middle of the night. I was twelve years old. My mother woke me as she tucked a beautiful Hispanic child with long, curly brown hair and huge, hungry eyes in my bed.

"This is Charlotte Marie," she said.

"Hi, Charlotte," I whispered. I thought she must be about three. Shivering and wide-eyed, she snuggled up next to me, and I whispered to her until finally we both fell asleep. The next morning I met her two older brothers. They were sitting at our kitchen table shoveling down cold cereal as though this were their last meal on earth. Both had ragged cigarette burns on their hands and arms, and the oldest's left eye was swollen almost shut. The boys seemed more wary than little Charlotte Marie, but all three were frightened and hungry for security.

My mother worked for a juvenile detention center, and she loved troubled kids. While I was young, our home often served as an emergency shelter for children who ended up in the custody of the state and who needed care at a moment's notice, day or night. It seemed like most of them did come in the night, kids who had been in immediate danger and were taken from their parents. They ate at our table, slept doubled up in our beds. None of them stayed long. They were all quickly placed in permanent foster homes.

It wasn't until I was an adult that I realized what the experience had done for me, how deeply I had been affected. At a very young age, I watched my mother reach out and provide security for one frightened child after another, with no questions asked when it came to loving. No child was too dirty, too poor, too far gone. Perhaps I couldn't help but grow up to do what I'm doing today.

Most of the children came and went without leaving the impression on me that Charlotte did. She was so elegant and dainty, and so receptive to kindness, that her image never left my memory.

✂

Fifteen years later, I saw Charlotte's face again in the lobby of the shelter. I was running to answer a phone call and caught myself just before crying out, "Charlotte, is that you?" It couldn't be Charlotte. Charlotte would have been older, but as I watched this young girl from where I stood talking on the phone, I could see the same elegance, the same daintiness about this child in the lobby, the same hungry eyes.

From the boxes and black trash bags surrounding her, it was evident that she was living in the lobby of the shelter, which was opened to families at night during winter months. Her hair, long and wavy and brown, tumbled around a sad face that looked up at me as I approached.

"My name is Maria," she responded as I introduced myself and held out my hand to her.

"Are you on the waiting list for a room at the shelter?" I asked.

"Yes," she whispered, glancing over at a man asleep on the floor.

"I'm a teacher here," I whispered back. "Why don't you come down to the classroom with me where we can talk and have a snack."

She glanced at the sleeping form again.

"Is that your father?"

She nodded.

"I think he'll be OK," I said. "I'll tell them at the desk where we're going in case he wakes up. We won't be gone long."

While we munched on crackers in the classroom, I learned that Maria was living with her father and his girlfriend, Alice, after being passed back and forth from relative to relative. They were staying in the lobby at nights until they could climb the long waiting list to get a room in the family shelter. Her father and Alice had picked Maria up at the bus depot last fall, and the three of them had been living with friends of his or in cheap hotels until just after New Year's. It was nothing really new to Maria.

"I was here once before," she said shyly, "when I was little."

I wrote down a few notes to myself after she left. Maria had a gentle, positive nature that wasn't typical for her age group and experience. Poverty had not destroyed her yet. A twelve-year-old child who has spent most of her life on the streets or among street people usually develops a way of thinking and living that is sometimes hard to cure. They adopt this sense of hopelessness, a feeling that it doesn't matter what they do right because nobody is going to notice. But Maria was different. Talking to her was like talking to an innocent little girl.

I want her in my class I wrote.

✂

A week or so later, Maria and her father got into a room at the shelter, and Maria started attending the School With No Name. She took over the classroom almost immediately, carving out her own space here where she was safe and life could be predictable. She tidied up library books on the shelves, and each day as she came in she would erase the old date in the corner of the chalkboard and write the new one, trying out some new handwriting stroke. After watching Maria draw, one of the teaching assistants gave her a sketch pad, and Maria carried it around everywhere she went. Once or twice a week she would stay after class to show me her pictures: houses and families surrounded by birds and animals. The faces she drew were always filled with sadness.

As the weather turned warm in early spring, the salsa music started up outside our windows. We had moved to the bottom floor of the shelter about a year before, and here, on sidewalk level, the music was loud. When the rhythms first started, Lori and I looked at each other across the room and began to dance. The kids shrieked with laughter; then they started jumping up to dance themselves. I pulled Maria up to do a couple of quick steps with me before I headed outside to ask the men on the sidewalk to turn it down.

The whistles and catcalls started up as soon as I stepped out the door.

"Hey, I'm trying to teach inside," I said.

"Ooo *mamacita*. Come dance with me."

"Hey, I'm only twelve, can I come to your school?"

"Hey, what can you teach me?" I could only imagine what they were saying in Spanish.

A group of Hispanic men always gathered around the flower box outside to dance and holler and sing. I liked them. They were happy, never seemed down or depressed, and they were polite in their own way. In the summers they would be out here all day in thongs and Levi's, crooning and joking.

"You've got to turn it down," I said again, smiling and pointing to the window.

"No *hablo!*" More Spanish.

When I finally got them to quiet down their boom boxes a few decibels, I turned and there was Maria.

"Do you know what they were saying to you?" she said with a sly smile as we walked back into the school.

"Was it naughty?" I asked as I threw an arm around her shoulder.

"Mmmhmm," Maria affirmed, and we both broke into laughter.

Maria was the brightest spot that whole spring, in the classroom where she was free to be her best self.

During the time she spent at the shelter, Maria's family consisted of Dad, his girlfriend Alice, and Maria. It wasn't the design or makeup of this unit that bothered me as the weeks passed; it was the distorted roles each member played. Maria helped with the laundry, cooking, and housecleaning, which wasn't so unusual, but she also shouldered the responsibility and worry for two adults living a fast-paced-but-going-nowhere lifestyle.

In an ideal family, parents make a commitment to love, protect, and provide security for the children they bring into this world. In Maria's family, the child assumed a reverse role, trying to act as parent to two adults who didn't know how to take care of themselves or their little bit of money. In Maria's case, the welfare money they received from the state to help care for Maria was regularly squandered on parties and binges. When her father was drunk, it became her job to see that everybody was warm enough and had someplace to sleep. She lived with two constant worries: what if they lost their place at the shelter because her father showed up drunk, and where would they go in three months when their time at the shelter ran out? Each time the family came close to having money saved for an apartment, it would mysteri-ously disappear. If you confronted either of the adults, each would blame the other's irresponsibility and drug or alcohol habit. Maria was caught in the middle, unable to discern the truth from the lies, unable to help herself or her father.

Their lifestyle left Maria alone much of the time. Many nights as I left, I saw her just standing around, waiting for her father and his girlfriend, doing nothing because there was nothing to do. She was alone when her dad and his girlfriend were out drinking. She was alone when they were high. Even though her father loved her, he was too consumed with his own needs to meet hers.

Substance abuse is one of the most critical issues facing the families that I serve. It is true that insufficient housing is a problem, as are insufficient education and a number of eco-nomic factors, but people can't take on housing or any other serious, long-term issue if they are dealing with a chemical dependency. And the greatest tragedy with substance abuse is that people lose their connection to their children. It happened with Anne Johnson, and it was happening with Maria's father. Meeting their need for the drug becomes more critical than meeting the needs of their children. It doesn't mean they don't love their kids, it doesn't mean they don't want to be good parents, but it means that they absolutely cannot live without their drug. It's not a choice for them—it's a necessity. And the children suffer.

Time and time again I watched Maria's beautiful, hungry eyes fill with tears as her adult role models would screw up and let her down again.

"Your dad will just have to learn from his experiences," I would tell her, wishing in my heart that for her sake he would hurry up.

✂

Maria's fear and disappointment caught me off guard one day in an entry in her writing journal. I usually write brief comments to the children in their journals, a response to their thoughts and feelings to validate them and let them know that someone is listening to them. Ideally, the writing serves as a daily source of therapy. Everyone needs to allow feelings to escape. If these children keep the anger, the fear, and the loss inside, they would become another generation of nonfunctioning people.

If the children want to keep what they have written private, they put a star at the top of the page, and I don't read the entry. Although Maria had drawn rows of stars across one page, it was evident that she didn't want me to miss the huge, bold letters she had written in response to the question of the day: "What could happen that would make you the happiest you've ever been?" Maria had written just four words: **"I WANT TO DIE."**

The next day, I was alarmed when Maria was not in class.

"Where's Maria?" a volunteer asked. It wasn't like her to

miss school. Fearing the answer, I cautiously asked the other students. A hush came over the circle. "Something's happened, guys. Should we talk about it," I suggested.

One student blurted out, "Her dad and his girlfriend got in trouble again. He got drunk and hit someone and they got kicked out of the shelter." I leapt to my feet.

"Have they already left?"

"Her dad has, but Maria slept here last night. She's packing their stuff now," another child said.

"Take over," I yelled to Lori, as I sprinted out of the classroom to find her. I could hear the thudding of objects being shuffled around and the stifled sobbing of a child when I approached Room 11. The door was propped open with an old tennis shoe so I stuck my head inside. Maria looked up from the garbage bag she had been stuffing full of clothes. Her eyes were red and her face naked with grief. She rushed to the door and wrapped her arms around me, choking back her tears. I took her in my arms, and she leaned her face against my shoulder.

"What happened, Maria?" I said.

"We got kicked out."

"Why?" I said. She didn't answer, but I knew why. Holding this child who reminded me so much of my own young daughter, I could feel my growing anger at Maria's father. My confusion mounted as I wondered what my role as a teacher and a humanitarian should be. I couldn't leave Maria to live on the street, yet I couldn't take her away from her father.

"I'll be fine," Maria reassured me, "It's not the first time. They'll find a way to make money so we can stay in a motel."

"You can't stay in a motel again, honey," I said, talking more to myself than her. "It won't be safe there, and you've got to stay in school."

Maria pulled away and wiped her eyes. "I have to hurry, my dad's real mad. If I'm not ready to go when he gets back, I'm dead."

"Tell me when you find out where you're going," I said, and she nodded. I pulled her close and hugged her tightly one more time before I walked away.

All the way back to the schoolroom I rehearsed my resignation speech. Nothing was worth another year of teaching in an environment so filled with loss and pain. The children have already lost their homes. When they move with their families to their cars or a shelter, they face losing friends and pets, schoolteachers, pride and self-worth. Their greatest loss is the chance to be children. Maria was headed back to a harsh, dirty world of drugs and violence, a world where she would watch the adults around her selling themselves in the name of providing shelter or a high. Though I knew Maria's father well enough to know he wouldn't barter his daughter to survive, others weren't so lucky. Perhaps her journal entry was not an uncommon thought for children who lived as she did.

As I walked, I wallowed in self-pity. I wasn't paying attention to where I was going and stumbled over a young child. As I bent over to pick him up and tell him I was sorry, I noticed Maria's father standing outside the shelter, trying to sell a few things that would bring quick cash for temporary shelter. I saw that Maria's boom box was up next, and all the anger flared up again.

As I stormed out of the building, I could hear Maria's father complaining loudly to the small crowd around him about the callousness of the shelter workers. They didn't care. They had kicked him out for no reason, just because they didn't like him. They always had their noses in business where they didn't belong. I had no business doing what I did next. But my body went on automatic pilot and I walked straight up to him.

"Maria isn't going with you. The streets are no place for that child," I told him. I was still a little teary from my meeting with Maria, and I could feel the anger and the fear competing in me.

"Just like I told you," he bellowed, working the crowd. "Going to try to tell me what to do with my own daughter." When he turned and started to get nasty with me, I couldn't hold my angry tears back any longer.

"I'm taking her home with me. When you get a place you can have her back," I managed to get out between sobs. My tears shook him, and he realized how serious I was. I had completely broken down, and he stood staring at this woman bawling in front of him on the sidewalk.

"What do you want to do that for?" he said, mildly subdued. I couldn't talk. He hung his head a minute, and the men standing around him on the sidewalk fell silent.

"I heard you've got kids of your own. Ain't you got enough to worry about?" I shook my head yes, then no.

"You mean it? You'll keep her just a little while, just till I get settled a little bit?" he asked, starting to choke up himself. I nodded again. He put a hand up to his eyes. "I'll tell her to bring her things to your room," he said. "Thank you." I put my hand on the boom box, and he let it go and turned into the shelter.

I hurried to my own office and dialed my husband. "Pam, is Greg in a good mood?" I asked his secretary, while I shoved Maria's boom box around to make space for it on my desk.

"I think so," she responded. "Why?"

"I need to bring a child home to live with us for a while." I could hear her sigh as she paged him. I never seemed to call to ask him to pick up a gallon of milk on the way home or to tell him he'd left his paperwork home on the bed.

"Hi, Hon," I said as Greg came on the line. "I have a really tough situation here. I may need to bring a child home for a little while."

"Only one?" he joked. "Sure, bring him home."

"Her," I said. "You're a good man, Greg." As I hung up the phone, I made a mental note to tell him how much I loved him when he got home.

Back in the classroom, I found the kids mesmerized by Lori's enthusiastic reading of "The Emperor's New Clothes." I wanted to sit on the rug and be anonymous for a few minutes, so I knelt quietly just outside the circle of children. Lori had just started the part where the emperor parades before his subjects in his handsome new robes (but in reality is totally naked). The children broke into uncontrolled giggles that we would be contending with the rest of the afternoon.

What a beautiful sound, I thought to myself.

I watched the door for Maria. It was another hour before she entered the classroom. No doubt she had waited until she could appear to be in control. Even with her world tumbling down around her, she wanted to appear calm. As I reached for her, she could no longer fight back the tears. I held her trembling body until she collapsed on the rug and fell asleep.

The other children were curious, compassionate, and envious that she was going to live with the teacher. Both she and I knew, though, that there was no reason in the world to envy the life Maria was living.

That evening, as we pulled into the garage, I warned her, "Our home gets crazy. The kids are coming and going every minute."

"I won't get in the way," she said.

"No, of course you won't," I chided, as I hugged her around the shoulders. "You're going to be right in the middle of it."

Maria seemed pleased with the fast pace once she got used to it—hurrying dinner, racing back and forth to the local high school to haul kids to and from swimming lessons, and then settling down to the nightly homework time. She was an easy child to have around. She didn't demand anything, and she enjoyed being part of a structured and child-oriented environment. She would get up early, make her bed, and put her things away in the corner. We teased our own daughter, Nichole, about being able to learn a few things from Maria. Maria did prefer chips and a Coke for lunch, habits you learn living in hotels and on the streets, and it started to bother us that she was too compliant, too anxious to please. I found her following me around picking up behind me as though she were brought to our home to work. Both irritated and saddened by her inability to be a kid, I tried to convince her that she didn't need to earn her keep.

My kids spent days coaxing Maria to shoot hoops with them or jump on the trampoline in the early spring weather. But Maria didn't know how to play, something that should have come to her naturally. She wanted to, but the concept was so completely foreign to her that she was more comfortable following me around the house, asking me what she could do to help. Finally, I had had enough. I gently took her by the hand and went to my closet to find my roller blades.

"I can't skate, Stacey. Please don't make me," she pleaded. But I caught a little half smile.

"It's time to learn," I told her firmly.

Maria giggled at the strange design of the skate with all the wheels in a line.

"How do you stand up?" she asked while I helped her buckle up the boots.

"You'll do great," I assured her.

"Don't laugh," she warned me.

We walked carefully to the door. Then, holding tightly to my arm, she began. With her inborn grace, Maria was a natural. As she stretched out her arms for balance and rolled down the driveway, we all cheered her. By the end of the afternoon, she was ready to proudly show off her new tricks: skating on one foot and turning a figure eight made up of wide circles.

I cheered inwardly as I watched Maria and Nichole sitting with their heads close together as they planned trips to the mall or the movies. They talked for hours, especially after the lights were out. Nichole showed Maria how to enter the childhood world of a young girl, a world full of youthful, happy dreams. Maria still dressed like a hardened street kid, clinging to her overalls and Raiders jacket, things that would cover her vulnerability. But I persuaded her to wear one of Nichole's dresses when she went with us to church, and Maria slowly came to accept her femininity, too, and recognize that she was a beautiful girl. I was seeing a troubled child turning into a confident young woman who was realizing for the first time that she deserved to be happy.

I checked every week with Maria's father to see what kind of arrangements he had come up with. He didn't appear to be making much progress. I found myself torn: I wanted to teach him to own up to his responsibilities, and at the same time I wanted to save his child from his bad choices. The contrast between the two lifestyles was starkly evident to Maria. Here she enjoyed security and constant activities as a part of a family instead of the hours of standing around outside the shelter and worrying about whether they would have one more day in their room. I knew she loved her father and missed him, but sometimes I still caught myself wishing he could just continue to fade further and further away.

But the inevitable call did come one day in early April.

"I got us a place," Maria's father told me. "I need to talk to Maria."

From across the room, I watched Maria talking on the phone. I wanted to get back on the line and demand some answers. Where was this place he'd found? What was he doing for work? I felt my stomach knot as Maria wrote down an address with a pen. She was going.

I was sick. That's the only way I can think to describe it.

"I wish you could stay for Easter," I told her, trying to sound cheerful while I helped her pack. What I wanted to say, what I wanted to shout, was, "I'm not finished." What kind of Easter was she going to have on the streets with her father?

I didn't trust him to provide for her, didn't believe he'd found anyplace for them to live where she ought to be. I did say all this and more to Greg.

"You're not her mother," he reminded me. I knew, too, that Maria missed her dad.

I kept leaving the room while she packed, trying to keep myself together. When I came in one time with an armful of clean clothes, Maria confided softly, "I miss my dad, but I'll miss you and Nichole and being here." I reminded myself that at least her father was taking the initiative of finding a home for his family. This was an important step.

"We're going to miss you, too," I said, while she sat on the bed, looking at the floor and spinning the wheels on one of my skates.

✂

We were silent during our drive to the west-side address Maria's father had given me. I was not sure exactly where I was going, but I knew this part of town was not for young girls. There were too many bars and too few homes. The flashing pink and blue sign reading "Zodiac Motel" told me that we had found Maria's new home.

"Oh, I get it," Maria said in disgust. "My dad's friends hang out here." I pulled up into the parking lot and stopped the engine. About thirty people stood in the parking lot, laughing, arguing, drinking. Not daring to look at Maria, I looked instead at my fearless sister Stephanie, who had accompanied us. She looked worried.

Dressed in the new, brightly colored clothes we had shopped for together, Maria climbed out of the car. While I helped her with her things, her clean, wavy hair glistened in the sunlight. Nothing about her belonged here. Still, as Maria's father hugged her tight, I could see the joy in Maria's face. Maria started chattering away, and he stood back to admire her clothes. I found myself fighting down hard feelings, trying not to be hurt that she was really excited to be here with her father in this dump after she had enjoyed the security of a home, new nice clothes, stability, and play.

I waved back to them as they stood in the parking lot together, waving to us as we drove off. Stephanie and I cried all the way home. The whole way I fought the urge to go back and get her, to bring her home and give her the things she needed to be a child—and to grow to be successful adult. Firmly I told myself, "Maria has a child's love for her father. You can't take this love for her daddy away from her." I understood that he was her father, her own flesh and blood, and I liked him as a person. I was not her mother— even if I wanted to be. But it made no sense to send this beautiful, talented child to live how she would have to live in an environment like that.

One of the hazards of my work is the pit in my stomach that aches at times like these. It's hardest when the children have to leave the shelter, and I know they are not going any-place better. More than half of the families at the shelter leave for a more stable environment, but many just repeat the cycle. They wind up back in the shelter, back in my classes, back in the same rut of poverty and bad luck or bad habits that keep them down.

It's gotten harder every year, as more and more families come to the shelter not because they are chronically tran-sient, but because the parents have lost a job or they can't find housing. Today, even though more and more people at the shelter leave every day for work, they are still home-less. One of hardest things about working with these people is not that they are difficult to love or to understand. It is watching them doing the best they can when their best still isn't good enough.

Our house felt empty when I returned. The gloomy feel-ing lingered like a ghost for weeks. Every time someone would find a trinket or sock that belonged to Maria, we remembered how it had been when she was here and where she had gone. This was always the hardest part of bringing children home—having them leave.

✄

The Saturday before Easter my children and I stopped by the shelter to pick up some extra Easter baskets that volunteers had brought to the school. We knew a family that had just left the shelter who wouldn't have a visit from the Easter Bunny, so the kids and I were going to substitute. Hurrying to my classroom, I didn't even see the small girl in the lobby who was at that moment trying to telephone my home.

"Mom, Mom, look," Nichole whispered. I looked across the room and saw a familiar face with hungry eyes.

Maria hurtled herself across the room and into my arms. "Oh Stacey, can I come with you? My dad got arrested last night and Alice didn't come home." Maria had spent the night alone in the motel and walked for miles to the shelter to call me.

"Let's go home," I said as we hugged each other. That evening the Easter Bunny raced to put together one more basket of goodies and to find an Easter dress for Maria to wear to the family brunch.

Maria's father agreed, again, to let Maria stay with us until he could provide a decent place for her, but a few weeks later he hit rock bottom. His money had run out and his girlfriend was tired of him and their downward-spiraling life together. She blamed him for wasting the money and he blamed her. They were both sick and sleeping outside in the weather that had turned wet and cool. He was finally ready to admit that he had a problem, and he realized that unless he made some radical changes he would end up dying—and he would lose Maria for good. One afternoon, he called and asked if we could get together.

We talked for hours. Like many substance abusers, he had been caught in a cycle of denial. It isn't often that the window of realization opens, when they are able to admit that something is wrong with the way they are handling their lives and ask for help. He was ready to listen to the truth.

"You know," I said bluntly, "you are destroying a very beautiful little girl."

"I know," he said humbly. "In fact, that's about all I know right now."

I continued. "Your need for a high has become more important than your daughter." Again, he nodded.

These were harsh and angry words, but I knew I wasn't dealing with a stupid man. This was a man who, in spite of anything else he may or may not have been, was kind and bright when he was sober.

"I love your daughter," I told him. "You might be the only person in the world who loves her more. I didn't bring her into my home to play games or manipulate you. Just to protect her while you got your act together."

"I know it," he said. His eyes glistened with tears. I reached out and hugged him.

"Then let's get you some help," I said.

The help we settled on was getting Maria and her father back to his family in the Midwest where he had a support system. There he could get a job, and life wouldn't be so hard in the small town where his mother and sister would be waiting with open arms for Maria. We rounded up travel funds through a volunteer group and an emergency assistance fund. Rescuing a father and child from their drug-infested environment was a good enough emergency for me. We purchased two one-way tickets on Greyhound, and I spoke to Maria's aunt over the phone to reassure myself that the family would work together to raise this beautiful child to reach her potential.

✂

When a request came in a few weeks for Maria's school records, I couldn't help but call the school in her new town. I explained Maria's situation to a counselor who had heard the whole story before and then begged her to look out for this particular child.

"She's pure," I found myself saying. "She's something special."

"She's coming to school on time. She's well dressed, happy, making friends," the counselor assured me. "Don't worry, we'll keep a good eye on her."

I hung up and settled back into my chair. I had told Maria good-bye at a little party we held for her at the house the night before she left. I excused myself from going to the bus station to see her off by saying I had a public speaking engagement. The real reason was that it would have been too hard. Then, after she left, I spent a quiet evening reminiscing and thumbing through the photographs we had taken of her while she lived with our family. They were pictures of Maria as I wanted to remember her, as I thought of her now, smiling and full of hope.

I love you, hungry eyes. ✐

✏ LESSON PLAN ✂

I Trusted You

Materials: Large paper, marker, crayons

Object: Teach children that we learn to trust one another by having positive experiences with our peers.

Activity:

1. Give each child a piece of paper. Instruct the children to write their names carefully in one corner; then invite them to draw a picture of anything that comes to mind. Give them time to do a good job.

2. Tell the children to pass their drawings to the person on their left.

3. Instruct the children to add to their neighbor's drawing.

4. Continue passing the pictures from child to child until each has contributed something and the drawings are returned to the original artists. Ask the children to quietly reflect on their drawing.

Questions:

1. Did you like your work better before you passed it to your peers or after? Allow time for each child to voice an opinion. For example: Dustin stands up and says, "I drew a beautiful city with my dream house right in the middle. It was good, and you ruined it."

2. Respond to the students' answers. Help the other students understand that by not respecting Dustin's drawing or by not being careful in the way they added to it, they hurt his feelings.

Close: Ask, How can we learn to be trustworthy so that our peers will want to share with us? Give the children a chance to talk about times in their lives when they trusted someone and that trust either was or was not respected.

Follow-up:

1. Give the children a second chance to show how we earn trust by caring about and respecting each other. Pass out more paper, etc.

✂

Now Josh, They're Waiting

Against my better judgment I finally consented to a "boy-girl" party for my daughter Nichole's twelfth birthday. I was feeling anxious about allowing her to grow up and struggling with the fear that I had not talked to her enough about the values I hoped she would take with her into young womanhood.

"Fear not," she said, assuring me that her first boy-girl party wasn't going to start her down the path of destruction and that she would always be my little girl. Still half-afraid and half-curious about her peer group, I helped her prepare the guest list and plan for the big event. Deep-dish pizza, pop and sparkling water, videos, with Mom and Dad confined to the kitchen.

The party was a hit as far as the kids were concerned. Had I not remembered my own pre-teen experiences I may have challenged their concept of a successful party. Success to a twelve-year-old isn't good food, good conversation, and fun. It's having the courage to invite all the boys that all the girls like so they can steal peeks at each other from across the room. The girls, all twelve of them, sat body to body on the couch scarcely looking at the boy guests. The boys, in turn, ate, joked, and horsed around loudly among themselves. That night I learned that my twelve-year-old was safe. The kids were still young. Their conversations were still about sports and French braids. My daughter was glad to just be twelve.

All that weekend as we planned the party beforehand and then shared the satisfaction afterward, I pondered the very different experiences two twelve-year-old children could have—for example, my Nichole and Josh, a student at the School With No Name.

Both were the same age, both eldest children. But there the similarities ended. Like most middle-class children, Nichole has had the luxury of being a child. Her greatest concern on her twelfth birthday was who to invite to her party. Will so-and-so like Amy? Will David really come? Most of the children at the shelter, like Josh, have skipped the childhood part of life. They learn early on to think in adult terms.

A kid like Josh worries about what he's going to eat, where he's going to sleep, what the family's going to do if Mom or Dad doesn't have a job before the time at the shelter runs out. The oldest in the family generally becomes the caretaker. He or she takes on the responsibility for the younger brothers and sisters, not in a baby-sitter way, but in a grown-up way, seeing to it that the younger ones are fed and warm and taken care of. Josh looked after his younger brothers like that, kept them as neatly dressed and clean as he was, got them up for breakfast and ready for school. It was Josh, too, who took the brunt of what was coming when things went haywire.

✂

By chance, Nichole and Josh did meet one day when I brought my children to work with me. I take them when I can because I want them to learn what I have learned, that we are meant to love one another and to serve one another and that we are not different. I also want them to share in the rich educational opportunities we have at the school, where we touch, smell, listen, look, and act upon learning rather than just reading about it.

When Nichole saw Josh swagger into the room, she went slack jawed. "Wow, Mom," she stammered. "He's cute."

"Cute" didn't begin to describe Josh.

Josh was tall, with dark, wavy hair and stunning hazel eyes. Dressed as fashionably as possible, with button-down

164

collars and the baggy pants that were in style, he carried himself with an air of coolness. He knew he was cool. I had learned from the kids who was nerdy and who was cool, and I knew he was definitely cool. And now Nichole obviously knew, too.

He had an arrogance about him that was sometimes annoying but was mostly quite funny. And I like the kids that society labels as "naughty." Josh was naughty at times, but in his heart he was very gentle. Like many naughty children, Josh had spunk and enough fight in him to battle his way ahead in his tough world, but at the same time he had a tenderness inside that allowed him to empathize with his peers.

I couldn't help but visualize him under the circumstances offered to my kids and to the kids in most of the middle-class neighborhoods in the city. With his zest for life, charisma, and brains, he could be anything he wanted. His great gift of compassion coupled sensitivity with sass. Usually the first to arrive, and the last to leave, Josh couldn't get enough of the stable environment the shelter school provided. He was the perfect kid, except for one minor problem.

Like clockwork, Josh's mother would come to the classroom to borrow Josh for a few moments every couple of days. I tried to emphasize to parents that even though this school was in the shelter, it was a public school and it needed to be treated like a public school. That meant minimal interruptions when class was in session. In a regular public school, parents would not be able to interrupt class to talk to their children or withdraw them from class for errands. Nor would the children have constant access to their parents while in school. I tried to follow this same policy with the expectation that my students would soon be in a regular school. The children were to learn to come to school on time, participate, and exercise a little bit of discipline. Parents needed to learn not to ask children to baby-sit or do the laundry, because their children needed to be in school.

At first, Josh's mother gave me the impression that she had so many responsibilities that she just needed help. I decided to let it go. Josh was a good enough student, and I thought perhaps his mother needed his help because she was illiterate and she needed him to read something for her, an occasional problem with my students' parents. In any case, I tried to ignore it.

"Where are you going, Josh?" I did ask once. "You're a kid. Let the grown-ups take care of the grown-ups. Your job is to be a kid. My kids are kids. I do my job and they do theirs."

Josh had only shrugged and I let it go—until the day we dissected the frogs.

This was the day Nichole met Josh. Although my own children were always enthusiastic about coming to school with me, they were as excited as my students to accompany me on the day I had planned for the class to dissect a bull-frog. All week I had been pounded with questions at home as well as from my students in class. "What day are we going to do the frog?" "Will there be enough frogs for everybody?" "Will they be dead already?"

We arrived early that day, and I asked Brandon and Nichole to help straighten a few things while I posted letters on the message board for some of the kids. As we were busily working, Josh strode through my door.

"Hey, Ms. Bess, let's *rejoice* now. I'm here," he announced before heading towards the bulletin board with a row of cows and the words "Out Standing in the Field!" across the top to collect some of his work from the day before. That's when I heard Nichole gasp. I glanced over and saw her jaw drop.

When he sauntered back over towards me, he stopped to peer at my hair.

"Grandma, your hair is getting really gray," he said.

"Josh, every single one of these gray hairs belongs to one of you kids. I used to be really pretty with dark hair, but since I started teaching you guys, this is what's happened," I retorted. "You can ask Nichole." The hair comments had become something of a ritual between Josh and me. Sometimes he would pluck a gray hair from my head and ask me, "Whose name is on this one?" His name was on plenty of them. He was a streetwise kid and didn't leave very many words unsaid in the classroom. Things he would never tell a teacher or think of saying in public school, he would come right out with in my class. When he did, I just tried my hardest to keep a straight face and was glad that he found the environment so safe that he felt he could freely express himself, knowing I wouldn't appreciate it but that he would still be allowed to stay.

"This is my daughter, Nichole," I said, enjoying watching my daughter blush as I made the introductions. "That's Brandon over there, my little boy."

"Hi," Josh said, flashing Nichole a wide grin, before he ambled over to the table where the other sixth-grade boys waited for him.

All the students wanted to dive right in and cut open the frog, even the girls. They didn't want to wait to hear about using the tools correctly or cutting carefully through the skin without disturbing the muscles so we could study the muscle structure. Everyone wanted to get right in there to see the organs. A few students looked a bit green, but Josh's face was eager and alive with interest.

Just as we were beginning, Josh's mother appeared at the door and asked to see him for a minute.

"But Mom..." he started to protest, but stopped at the look in her eyes.

"Let's go," she hissed. "Now, Josh. They're waiting."

"Who's waiting?" I wondered. As I looked at Josh and his eyes met mine, I could feel his embarrassment as his childhood power was stripped from him in front of his teacher and peers. I winked at him to let him know that I understood and it was all right if he had to leave. Nichole watched him go and asked me before we left that day why he hadn't come back. Something wasn't right.

All that night I kept hearing, "Hurry up, they're waiting." Who could be waiting? I asked myself over and over with no logical conclusion. I promised myself the next morning I would take a moment with Josh to get some answers.

But the following morning there was no Josh. By 9 o'clock I was getting a strange feeling that something was wrong, so I hurried to Room 22 where his family was staying. I saw a small figure at the door, shoulders slumped, head bowed low. As I approached, the head raised to reveal the tear-stained eyes of a devastated child.

Twelve-year-old boys who are cool don't cry, and they don't hold their teacher in public as tightly as Josh held me. But when a twelve-year-old boy is responsible for letting the family secret out of the bag to the police, which means that his whole family may be separated, he may suddenly be willing to let his teacher hold him in her arms while he sobs for anyone in the world to see.

Through his tears, he told me good-bye. Later I found out what happened.

The police had apprehended Josh with drugs in his possession, and the family had been asked to leave the shelter. I knew they weren't for himself; he didn't take drugs. If he had said the drugs were his, his family might not have been caught in the backlash, something he might have done, had he thought of it. But he was young and frightened, and instead of making up some complex story for the police, he admitted that he was the drug runner for his parents.

As the family frantically packed, Josh stood in the hall watching the preparations that would tip his life upside-down again. I could tell he felt it was his fault for being caught and that his parents were not letting him feel any different. By ignoring him, acting as though he would not be going with the family, they were punishing him for being

168

careless and getting them thrown out of the shelter.

"I'm sorry, Stacey," he sobbed over and over, while I held him and his family ignored both of us. "I'm sorry. I'm sorry."

I haven't seen Josh since, although I did hear of him through a colleague of mine, Michelle, who was visiting a neighboring public school and overheard a couple of administrators discussing what to do with the "child from hell." Michelle wondered what hoodlum had earned that title, and then in the office she saw Josh sitting stiffly on the couch, his face a careful blank.

When he saw Michelle, his mask shattered. As she bent down to hug him, he started to cry. "I miss my old school. I miss Stacey's class. She liked me."

I did like Josh, and I think that if a child as smart and as caring as Josh is now a "child from hell," it is because nobody took the time to nurture him. It is more a matter of circumstance than character. Josh and too many other twelve-year-olds have their chances decreased, not because they are bad or destructive, but simply because they lack the opportunities and the encouragement children require. Children like Nichole have parents and teachers who have taught and encouraged her to think ahead, to problem solve, to be self-motivated; who have helped her with homework, corrected bad behavior, and supported her in swimming and dance lessons. When she is interested in something, we are there to help her find and develop her gifts and talents. When she has questions or worries, we are there to talk about them.

It is possible that Josh will never know these things or ever have these chances. He will not receive these same opportunities for growth. Among the middle class, we find the perpetuation of the America dream: my kids will do at least as well as I did. Among the homeless and the poor, the inheritance is often a legacy of poverty and failure if the family has lived this way for generations. These kids will step up a rung, too; they will usually progress and be a little better off than their parents, but they will never catch up without intervention—especially the intervention of education. If kids don't know how to make choices and how to think critically, they don't have a chance.

Because of these differences, Nichole simply has a much better chance at success—she will find her talents, she will discover what she can do for her world. But there are other avenues to save Josh. We are fond of saying, if the family can, the family should. But let us also say, if the family does not or cannot, we will. We may expect other organizations, other agencies, other families to step in and save these children. But when we see that they do not, instead of accepting this, we have to say, I will do my best to make up for what is missing here. ✏

September 1

Dear Diary: Today we had show and tell. I didn't have anything to show. We put our dog to sleep. I thought we were supposed to learn our phone number in kindergarten. Do we have one? I like it here. We learned about shapes and colors. Dad'll be proud. Can we call him at the prison tonight?

P.S. Teacher asked us where our secret hiding place was. I don't have one, but Dad does. I told my teacher that he hides his needles in the toolbox.

McKenzie's
Lesson of Love

"Good morning, Teach!"

I heard those heartwarming words over and over again as I made my way through the crowded street to the foyer of the Family Shelter.

"That's a real nice baby girl you have there. Do you bring that beautiful little thing to work with you every day?"

"Yep," I replied, "crazy as it sounds, I sure do."

❄

A few weeks earlier I would not have dreamed of that response because I had never dreamed of bringing my baby with me to the school. I had agonized for months over the choice I believed I had to make between staying home to be with my baby or continuing to teach the children at the School With No Name. I had dedicated six years to these homeless children's needs and been their advocate statewide. Now I was passionately in love with my newborn child and firm in my belief that she needed to spend the first year of her life close to her mother. Yet I loved these children at the school, too, and couldn't ignore the nagging feeling that I wasn't finished there yet. It was a real and a painful dilemma.

One day Gail, my colleague who ran the clinic for home-less families, spoke the unthinkable: "Bring your baby with you to work. Newborns sleep most of the day. It will be good for the children to see some healthy mother-child interaction, and she'd be OK because babies come with a built-in immune system."

I didn't care how healthy her immune system might be. The staff saw to it that the shelter was kept clean, but what about some of the people who were constantly tracking in and out, or even the germs from a classroom full of kids? Even more unthinkable was the danger of drive-by shootings, the drug dealing, and the general atmosphere of anger and violence that characterizes the neighborhood. My head responded to the whole idea with a resounding NO! but my heart vetoed the logic with a powerful and inexplicable YES!

A tremendous weight lifted off my heart the minute I made that decision and I felt peace again, at last. I also felt a strange excitement as though something unusually good was about to happen. Explaining to my family would be another matter. The line that seemed to characterize Greg's response to and patience with my work was, "Do what you have to do." Taking McKenzie to the shelter with me was a little different than working late or boarding children in the house for a little while. Still, my mind was made up. I looked at McKenzie Anne, my beautiful, innocent newborn sound asleep in her carrier, and said to her, "Sweetheart, you are about to become a schoolgirl."

McKenzie and I began teaching together on October 13, 1992, when she was exactly eight weeks old. The sky was a crisp autumn blue and the air full of the noise of downtown, traffic and shouting. I approached the school that day with a strange combination of feelings: apprehension, excitement, joy, and fear. It seemed appropriate that the first person to greet me seconds after I reached the foyer of the family shelter was Sarah, a longtime resident of the streets. She was about fifty with a large build, short hair, and a tongue as bitter and sharp as any venom. Crowds parted when she appeared. She wore the look of a tired old woman who just wouldn't give up until something gets better.

Sarah hung around the shelter a lot, and we had found each other the winter before when she had been raising hell in the hall of the shelter trying to find a coat. After she found out I was pregnant, Sarah would spot me from blocks away and would yell at the top of her lungs, "Hey fatty, when you gonna have that baby?" Then she would jog to my side to place her grubby hands on my belly to talk to "our baby" as she called her.

As Sarah approached me on my first day back with the baby, my family's words of caution were pounding in my head: "Don't let just anyone hold the baby. Please be careful about germs."

Sarah spoke with uncharacteristic tenderness and low volume. "I've been so worried about our baby. How is she doing?" I immediately felt Sarah's longing for the love she had tasted so little of in her life. Guardedly, in a solemn tone that told me she didn't expect the request to be granted, Sarah asked to hold my McKenzie Anne. All concerns flew out of my mind, and the last thing I cared about was the dirt-gray color of what used to be her white coat. I simply couldn't deny her hunger to feel what love was like. As I unwrapped McKenzie from her blanket, I noticed that Sarah's eyes were beginning to fill with tears. I placed my baby's snuggly, warm body in Sarah's arms and watched as the magic began. She held the baby over her shoulder and wept as McKenzie nuzzled her neck with her tiny, soft, tickley mouth.

The meanness of our surroundings disappeared, and for the moment everything was beautiful for Sarah, the baby, and me. A power bigger than I confirmed the choice to share this baby with these people who had become such a big part of my world. At that moment I began to sense the importance of what McKenzie Anne could do here and knew she would be fine while she did it. Without any words at all, she would teach the healing power of love.

As I stepped into the schoolroom, the children were anxiously waiting. I had told them the day before that McKenzie would be coming with me to class and let them know what I expected of them. The smell of disinfectant filled the air, and the stacks of papers and books on the counters looked to be a little straighter than usual, but that didn't account for the new and different feeling in the room. It was as though angels were present to watch over my littlest angel.

"We been lookin' forward to this for a long time, Miss Stacey," said one little girl as she tugged at McKenzie's pink blanket. "We're gonna be real good for the baby so that she don't get afraid."

As I began the formal introduction of McKenzie Anne Bess, the room fell silent. No chairs squeaked. Nobody whispered in the back or kicked anybody. No one yawned. The children's concern for the baby was evident. Tenderness, usually so well concealed in these tough, streetwise kids, had surfaced in surprising quantities. To build trust and get the children to let down their walls and let love in invariably took time and work, but McKenzie accomplished it instantly, effortlessly.

"She will be our mascot of love," I told them, surprising myself. "If life gets unbearable, all you will need is a snuggle from baby McKenzie and all the bad feelings will go away." In the days to come, the children spent many contented moments rocking and snuggling the baby. Even the boys would find reasons to take a turn to hold her and caress her soft little arms.

✀

McKenzie's extended visit wasn't the first time we had brought love into the classroom by taking in special guests. Lori, my teaching assistant, came in one day shaking the rain from her umbrella to tell me that an old woman and two twin boys were sitting outside the shelter in the rain.

"What are they doing out there?" Lori said, peeling off her wet jacket.

"It's a mother and her first-grade boys," I said without looking at her. I knew they were out there. The boys were Travis and Trent, filthy, but beautiful, shy, curly-haired boys. I had met the family earlier, and I was trying not to think about them out in the rain. "Their room won't be ready until five, and they can't loiter in the lobby."

"What are they going to do?" Lori wanted to know.

"I can't do anything about the rules," I snapped. Lori dropped it for the moment, but she and some of the children took turns going to the door for a look outside, where it kept on pouring. Finally, about eleven o'clock, Lori came in and cornered me.

"Stace, they're drowning out there," she wailed.

"Let's bring them in the back door," I said. "Hurry up."

Lori snuck the family in, and we hid them in the classroom for the rest of the day. The kids loved having a secret and went around the room whispering and peeking out the door to make sure no one was coming. We got coffee for the mother and had the boys wash up in the bathroom. The children fed the boys out of the snack cupboard and put videos on for them to watch, while their mother rocked stiffly in our rocking chair, thanking the children as they went by. The class had fun being conspirators, and I still remember Travis, one of the twins, spread-eagle and dead to the world in the beanbag chair while *All Dogs Go to Heaven* played on the TV overhead.

It was more than just fun and being naughty by bending some of the rules, though. The kids were giving, sharing. I don't remember any fights that day. I don't remember any tears or hurt feelings or tantrums. It was a good day, with a peaceful feeling in the air. The days with McKenzie in the room were a lot like that.

✂

For the next eight months, McKenzie Anne spent many of our hours at the school contentedly strapped to the front of my body where she could hear my heartbeat and my voice as I interacted with my class. I felt secure knowing that she was warmly tucked against me, and she must have felt secure because she never cried or fussed. Miraculously enough, my baby was not sick a day that whole year.

Among the unexpected benefits of bringing McKenzie to work were the reactions of my students' mothers. When they asked me about the baby, I could explain that I felt very strongly about their children's educational needs and just as strongly about mothering. I found that parents showed much more interest in their kids' learning environment while I was there with the baby. Mothers especially trooped in and out of the room freely to take a look. This, in turn, benefited their children. The minute a mother would step inside the door her children would beam with joy that she had been curious enough to investigate their classroom.

Of course, the most profound impact of McKenzie's presence was on the children themselves. Normally the school can get pretty noisy, and angry outbursts are common—hitting, tipping over chairs, throwing things. Anger at the lack of control they have over their lives is typical among the children at the shelter school, and some let their emotions out violently. When you teach four or more grades of students who feel this way and they are all in the same room, the atmosphere can be supercharged with hostility.

To my surprise, after explaining how I felt about my baby the children all agreed on some ground rules, such as keeping the noise level to a minimum. I thought it would take a miracle for the children to show enough discipline to be even relatively quiet—but miracle we got. You couldn't hear a pin drop, but the kids were careful and quick to call for quiet when the volume started creeping up. The unkind words and angry outbursts seemed to diminish, too, maybe because we all had someone else to think about besides ourselves.

As time went on and new children joined the class, the veterans taught them the importance of never being loud or doing anything to frighten the baby. For those few months while McKenzie was in the classroom, the room was consistently filled with an unusual love and peace—McKenzie's most important gift to all of us. Because of that gift, it was a year that none of us will ever forget.

The children had a million questions about this little child's growth before she was born—questions that never seemed to stop. So I got permission from each parent and brought a poster from my doctor explaining how she grew inside of me. We learned together the stages of development: when the eyebrows were formed, when the tiny fingernails appeared, and when the fetus's ears were developed enough to hear noises from outside the mother.

The effects of drugs and alcohol on the fetus came up time and time again. The horror stories my students told were enough to make everyone sick. The firsthand knowledge they had of what each street drug did to the unborn child shocked even my somewhat calloused sensibilities. As they told their stories, I knew some of the faces I was watching belonged to children living the stories they were telling me due to the addictions their mothers had had when they carried them. The thought made me both angry and weary. These kids knew the facts about drugs as well as anybody, but it isn't enough just to know. I pulled a little blond boy named Kyle close for a hug, thinking that what these kids really deserve to be taught is to value life, to value themselves and their potential, and to be given a chance to find happiness.

I sensed from the first that McKenzie would teach us all some lessons, but I only began to get a glimpse of the real impact she was having on the children when I sat alone one Friday afternoon to catch up on their journal entries.

Kyle wrote simply, "Baby McKenzie makes me feel safe."

John wrote about my lesson on the effects of drugs and alcohol on our bodies. "I can't believe how the alcohol and drugs pass on to the baby," he wrote. "It makes me sad to think that they get high even if they don't want to." As I read further in his entry I was pleased to learn that John had come to value the fetus and its miraculous growing process. He concluded with, "I will be sure to protect my unborn child from drugs." I responded with a little photograph of McKenzie taped to the page and a note: "This will help remind you how beautiful life is. I'm pleased with your choices."

Almost all of the kids had written something about the baby's growth during the past few weeks, but tucked in between were comments indicating how the baby was filling previously unmet needs. Lana wrote about trust. "No one has ever trusted me with their baby except my teacher. After lunch yesterday she let me change her diaper. It was a little gross, but I was surprised how easy it was. I think the baby smiled at me."

Dirk's entry was a poignant reminder of the abuse he was so familiar with: "I kept looking at my teacher's baby yesterday. She had a really red mark on her face. It kept bothering me. I know she wouldn't hit her but I had to ask. I asked and she wasn't mad. She laughed and showed me that it was only a lipstick kiss that had been smeared."

McKenzie remained a favorite topic throughout that year. Even so, I was surprised toward the end of the year when I was again reading from their journals on a Friday. The topic for Friday's writing was "What Makes you Happy?" I expected McKenzie Anne Bess to be one of the topics but was surprised that ten out of twelve students wrote about watching me with the baby. One little girl wrote:

> My teacher is funny.
> She really likes her baby
> You can just tell by the
> way she kisses her all over
> and leaves lipstick marks on her head.
> Watching her makes me happy.

At the bottom she added:

> I wish somebody would have loved me like
> that when I was little.

In one short line, this lonely little girl summarized the aching, longing wish of every one of these homeless children, and every member of the human family: to be loved all over, to be loved completely, to be loved unconditionally. I had tried to give that kind of love to them, but it was McKenzie Anne who succeeded best—in her pure, trusting response to the children, she gave them glimpses of love, precious moments when they actually experienced what that kind of love feels like. I knew at that moment that all the risks and all the hard work that year had been more than worth it. At the same time I knew sadly, surely, my classroom would never be the same without her. ➥

The Greatest Love of All

I had been watching my students come and go for almost six years before the day I found Bryan hiding under my desk during reading time and asked if I could join him for a little while. During reading time, the kids could be found just about anywhere. They stretched out on the miniature blue couches, curled up on the beanbag, or crawled under a table. I liked to wander around the room and listen while they read aloud. It gave the kids some personal attention and a chance to show off while I did some evaluating and offered a little extra help. Bryan was usually eager for an audience.

"No!" he yelled at me this time. "Go away!" Burying his tear-stained face in his book, he began crying again. I knelt by him, slowly running my fingers through his thick hair. I had found over the years that the environment in the school is safe enough that eventually he would feel secure in releasing his anger. He did—in a kick to my leg that left a bruise halfway up my thigh.

Earlier that day, I had written on the board "I am __" and instructed the children to fill in the blank with an emotion and then use color words and action words to describe that emotion. The hope was that they would remember the parts of speech while they evaluated some of their feelings. Bryan's emotion was anger, his colors black and red. He wrote action words that told a story: "Packing, driving, yelling, afraid."

I nursed my leg and left Bryan alone for the rest of the day until he attacked another child then ran as I tried to grab him. We wove in and out of chairs—with my sixth-grade boys cheering Bryan on—until I finally cornered him under a computer desk. He wouldn't come out when I asked him to, so, with the rest of the class gathering around or craning their necks to watch, I started counting down a warning.

"One. Two. Come on Bryan." I don't usually get to three, though sometimes we have a long two-and-a-half. I went to four this time, hoping to lighten up the tense situation. Bryan stayed put, hugging the wall behind him with one hand wrapped tightly around a leg of the desk, his face puffy and red from crying.

"All right," I said. Enough was enough. I reached under the desk to pull him out, being careful to stay clear of his legs. He started thrashing around, and as I struggled to get a good grip, he sunk his teeth into my arm.

"You don't need stitches," Gail told me as she finished patching me up in the clinic. My arm stung from the antiseptic. "Why did he bite you?"

"I don't know. He's been upset all day," I said. "I've been hit, kicked, yelled at, slapped, thrown up on, but I don't think I've been bitten before." It was only half funny.

"I guess that makes today something special," Gail joked. "Congratulations."

Back in the classroom, I collapsed into my chair and examined the bandage on my arm. On my desk I saw a carefully folded note addressed to me from Bryan:

"I'm sorry I was angry today. I'm moving."
                                                Bryan

Now I could put the pieces together. For three months, Bryan had found a home, of sorts. He slept in the same bed every night, went to school every day, made friends. He was just starting to get settled. Now he was leaving again; he was going to lose everything he had found. Homeless children feel the same loss that you and I feel when faced with moving, a divorce, or the death of a loved one. Most of us experience serious loss only a few times in our entire lives. I have had kids come through who have lived in seven different states in one year. They need two yards of yarn and a dozen thumbtacks just to show the class where they have been on the big map at the front of the classroom. Homeless kids whose families are transient can move seven or eight times in one year, leaving friends, pets, stable surroundings, family members. No wonder Bryan was angry.

I should have seen it coming. I had done this long enough that I had begun to expect and understand the outbursts that sometimes cropped up near the end of a child's stay. I missed the signs with Bryan and had to learn the lesson over again. Maybe I was losing my edge. The average burnout rate in a job like mine was something like two years, and I had been here six. I had heard a staff member say once, as one of my older students left, "We can carve his name on a bed post for him. He'll be back within two years." I didn't want to stay if I got like that. Some people told me it wasn't even a matter of *if*—it was only a matter of *when*.

As I sat there taking stock, the noise in the hall outside died down and the light faded in the classroom. I couldn't count the number of times I had wanted to quit. You get tired of wondering if you have done anything constructive. Wondering if you can penetrate one more barrier. Sometimes the kids are so far behind, you just about lose hope. And mostly, it's downright exhausting. But almost immediately when the thought of leaving tugged at my brain, a little child would tug at my sleeve, or I would hear a familiar voice yelling "Hi, Teach," from the street, and I'd be yanked right back into why I stayed.

The kids came needing so much, so hungry for love, for learning, and for any little bit of childhood we could give them. If you wanted to be loved in life, all you had to do was come here and give a little bit, and you would be smothered in it. If you wanted to change the world, here was a world that certainly needed changing. If you had scars that needed healing or wanted to forget your own troubles, you could come here and try to patch up somebody else's. I had seen it work over and over again with the volunteers who walked in hesitant and afraid and left with friends they would never forget. There is a peace that comes with giving, with service. Underneath the chaos, the noise, the naughtiness, and the anger, there was a comforting spirit in our classroom, and it was generally a happy and a safe place to be.

I could tell, though, that my time was coming. I could give it at least one more year, but I owed my family, too. And as much good as I convinced myself that I was doing, I wondered what else was out there. I would never abandon the children, but maybe it was time to move the battle to a different arena—administration, more speaking and advocacy work, something.

I had gotten stiff sitting in my chair, and I stood up to stretch. The dim light outside the windows told me I was late getting home—really late. I reread Bryan's note and worried suddenly that he might not be in class tomorrow so we could talk about it. That was another reason I had stayed—in case any of my kids came back looking for me. Jenny did, when she had her baby. And Zach, the golden-haired boy from my first class at the School With No Name, had just left after a visit. I was beginning to accept that I couldn't be there always for everyone, but still Zach had become my symbol of hope. When I really started to wonder if it was worth it or began to lose hope, I could think of Zach, a student and friend from my first days at the School With No Name.

His story is best told with some of his own words.

✂

My name is Zach. I was eleven when I first came to the family shelter. I came from Arizona with my dad. I've traveled all over, but this was my first time ever coming to a shelter. Before we came to the shelter we stayed in our car for a couple of days because we didn't know about the family shelter. I'd been to about twelve different schools. Some of the teachers were nice, but I didn't like any of my science teachers, they were all mean.

When I first met Stacey I didn't like her. She expected us to be in school, or she came looking for us up and down the viaduct, knocking on the car doors and our rooms, yelling for us to get up. I didn't want to get up. I had my troubles with her. I wouldn't come to class sometimes at first, but then we became really good friends, and she really brought my self-esteem up. She kept on telling us you can be what you want to be. Stacey used to do fun things with us. She used to sing songs and read us stories, things like that.

✂

Any mother would have taken Zach for her son. He was eleven when we met, an all-American boy with china-blue eyes who was cool and everybody's friend. All the children flocked around him. Two adjectives that describe Zach are gentle and strong. His gentleness is expressed through words of love for the people and objects that have provided meaning in his life. His strength lies in his ability to reveal his most vulnerable feelings and his undying hope for a brighter future. Together, we described the qualities we liked in each other through poetry.

MY TEACHER
My teacher is a lady bug who is soft and gentle
    all the time
She is a screwdriver driving you to
    meet your goals
My teacher is a harp playing soft and
    quiet with style
She is herself, you can't compare her with anyone
My teacher is a violet that speaks loud
    but is so soft it heals us all

ZACH

Zach is a strong polar bear cub,
  hungry to be nourished by the warmth of a
  caring world
He is a power jigsaw,
  carefully cutting away the rough edges
  of his outer shell

Zach is a shiny gold guitar
  filled with a musical power to change the world
He is a super child
  surviving the brutal realities of homelessness

Zach is a seedling experiencing the warmth of spring,
  with much hope for a firm foundation
  and a budding future.

✄

The shelter school was a new experience for me because the teachers had more time to sit down with the kids. They helped you more. They didn't just sit there and give you work; they tried to build up your self-esteem and give you confidence in yourself by telling you that you could do things and you could be somebody when you grew up.

The time I spent in Stacey's class was different, and if I hadn't been in her class I may not have graduated from high school. I think she's the one who brought me out, saying that I could be what I wanted to be, I could do what I wanted to do, and she taught me that staying in school was probably the best thing for me.

✄

One Friday afternoon, maybe a month after I had started at the School With No Name, I was frantically cleaning, trying to make the 12x12 closet look more like a classroom. Feeling overwhelmed and a little frustrated, I sat on a stool and leaned my back against the chalkboard. Before me lay the jumbled sea of battered desks, shelves of cinder block and planking along three of the pasty-yellow walls, and the matted carpet that was always muddy. I was learning that it wasn't the physical structure that makes a school a school; it is the people who love the children, the nurturing, the motivating, and the passing on to one another the love of learning. Still, I wondered what it would be like to teach in a room where you could open the blinds and not find the windows smeared with grime or blood.

I took a deep breath. "Make the best of it," I was telling myself when a loud pounding at the window startled me.

"Can I come in and help?" Zach said, poking his head in the doorway. His smile was wide and friendly. He slipped into the room and stood with his head cocked to one side under a new fitted baseball cap, his thumbs hooked in his pockets. Recognizing that this was a rare kid who wanted to maintain his coolness and yet befriend his teacher, I accepted his invitation.

On that first Friday together, we worked for a while; then Zach went out and brought back a Coke for each of us. When he returned, he propped his feet up on my desk and began to fill me in on his life. His dad didn't have much money, so they kept leaving one town after another in search of better pay. Zach described a life of unending travel with his father, of having to meet new friends wherever they decided to stop for a while. He told me that he had to get along with new kids because he was "different and new all the time."

"When I was two, my mom and dad got a divorce," Zach said. "Me and my brothers were too small to understand what was going on. But for some reason she kept my brothers and gave me to my dad."

This stunned me. As the mother of a three-year-old son at this time, I couldn't imagine a mother being able to let go of her child not knowing if she would ever see him again.

"Have you seen her since?" I said.

"No," Zach answered, "she didn't want me. I looked too

much like my dad." He said it so matter-of-factly that I knew it was a well-practiced front meant to hide his feelings.

"Are you angry?" I asked softly.

"No," he said, "but sometimes I wish things could be different. Dad works a lot. We have to live, you know. He needs a life of his own, too, so sometimes I get lonely." I knew that Zach had a great dad, and Zach was aware of the difficulties his father was facing. But that understanding didn't make the loneliness or all of the other emotions less painful.

"What would you fix about your life if you could?" I asked him. Zach sat up straight to say something important.

"I love my dad, but I don't like to move so much and leave people just when I finally get used to them. I get sad and mad for a while. Then just when I get better we leave again."

What Zach was experiencing and explaining, I would come to find out, was the loss process. It was the same thing Bryan was going through years later when he bit my arm.

Zach's feelings about loss, abandonment, loneliness, and a sense of security can all be read about in the research that has been done on poverty. But here was a kid who was experiencing firsthand what can happen to create a child who does not feel *whole.* Zach was lucky because, unlike many of my students, many vital elements were secure in his life. He had a loving father and a strong sense of the importance of learning. Zach's father put his son's needs first, and Zach never went without food or a warm place to sleep. Still, many necessary components were missing. I found myself wondering as he left if we as a society could pick up the missing pieces of the puzzle and create a whole child. Isn't that our responsibility?

✂

What made me feel that Stacey was somebody important to me was the feeling I got from giving back to her when she went into the hospital for cancer. While she was there, a girl named Barbara, who was in the class, and I thought, "We'll go down

*there and visit her." We went to the mall to buy her presents
and get-well cards, and we got kicked out because the security
guard thought we should be in school. He didn't know our
teacher was in the hospital. When we got to the hospital room,
Stacey and her mom were surprised to see a couple of her students. Stacey opened her eyes and there we were.*

✂

Near the end of my first year at the School With No Name,
I was diagnosed with thyroid cancer. My first response was to
put up a brave front for my class. But I began to realize that
they needed to know how I really felt. I knew instinctively
that the whole situation could actually create a closer kinship
with them. They were no strangers to anger, fear, and frustration. I had an audience that would understand what I was
feeling, and they had a right to know.

So I had a very open and frank discussion with them.
They wanted to know how I knew I had cancer, and I
explained that because I wanted to have another baby, I had
gone to the doctor to be sure I was healthy. The doctor, feeling my neck, had discovered lumps. I invited the children
one by one to come up and feel the lumps in my neck.

"Does the cancer make you afraid?" April asked soberly.

"Yes, I am afraid," I replied honestly.

I explained to them what cancer was, that cancer
spreads, that the doctor wouldn't know until he opened up
my neck how extensive the cancer was, and that I would let
them know what he found out. I didn't gloss over the problem, and I told them exactly what the doctors were going to
do to me when I went in for surgery. There was genuine caring in their voices when they said, "You'll be OK, Miss Stacey.
We know you'll be OK."

As I left school on the last day before my surgery, one of
the children's father stopped me at the door and handed me
a shiny blue piece of paper.

"Good luck," he said, wrapping his big arm around my

shoulders and pulling me in close like a buddy. "We want you back." I stood there stunned, smothered in the folds of his big, musty coat. This wasn't behavior as usual for the men around the shelter.

"Thanks," I said. It was all I could think of. After he left, I looked down at the paper where he had written "Jesus Loves You" and "When one door closes, another one opens some-where else" with a picture of two doors. A strange sense of reassurance filled the place where a lot of my anxiety had been and I felt a fierce determination. Now that these people and I had found each other, I wasn't about to leave.

The door that was closing was the door to my healthy body. Cancer wasn't one of those things that ever seemed to go away, and I would live with the thought of it nagging at the back of my mind for the rest of my life. I was angry, and I was afraid. The doctors told me again and again that my condition was treatable and we had caught it early. I was supposed to be lucky, but I didn't feel lucky. I spent every minute I could before my scheduled surgery with Greg, Nichole, and Brandon. The kids at the school crept into my thoughts more often than I would have imagined, too. I had a huge envelope stuffed with handmade get-well cards and a lot of reasons to live, I thought, as I prepared for surgery. I had a lot of work to do.

The door that opened, a door of understanding, would be a door that let me into the world of the children at the school. I understood fear better now than I ever had. I under-stood coping with a devastating situation. I knew denial and anger. The threat of cancer was the threat of losing every-thing I loved. This was the world my students and their par-ents lived in perpetually.

As I woke in the recovery room I could sense that the shadows moving in and out of the lights above me were peo-ple standing over me. Through the haze, I could hear as my mother spoke first.

"Stace, you're OK, and that makes a couple of people here pretty relieved." I looked over, trying to focus, and saw Zach and Barb from the school. Their arms were loaded with gifts and their eyes shiny with tears. I smiled and forgot all about my family standing around my bed.

Zach leaned over me and asked in a tight voice, "You okay, Teach?"

"I'm okay, Zach," I managed to get out before I drifted back to sleep, feeling very lucky to be surrounded by people who understood love.

My mother told me later that Zach and Barb had been waiting at the hospital for hours, pacing around the recovery room, hounding every doctor or nurse they could corner about my condition and care.

"I don't even know how they got in," my mother confessed. "It was supposed to be just family." Zach and Barb wouldn't admit much to my mother, just that they were two of my students from the school and that they had no substitute teacher yet for afternoon classes while I was in the hospital. They said they just wanted to make sure I was OK, so they decided to take the bus up to the hospital to check things out. How they got the gifts, heaven only knows—I didn't feel it was my place to ask. All I knew is that they had been there with me.

✄

I've kept in touch with Stacey in a strange way. When I moved to Alaska I didn't call her like I did right after I left the school. Then one night I was listening to Whitney Houston and I heard her sing "The Greatest Love of All," and I just thought of Stacey. Even though it was midnight, I got on the phone and I called her.

✄

One day both Zach and his dad barreled through my door, beaming with excitement. Zach's father had landed a good job at the south end of the valley.

"Things are lookin' up," he said. "This new boss of mine is really a great guy. He owns the company and really cares about his people and their families."

"That's great news!" I hugged them both. In an environment of continual disappointment, I was elated to hear a parent express hope. Homelessness brings with it the threat of getting stuck in the cycle. If you don't have a phone, address, car, or appropriate clothing, it can be next to impossible to land a decent job. Zach's father and many others who find themselves homeless had also been up against negative stereotypes about their ability or willingness to work; yet many of the guests at the family shelter get up and go to work every day. Many who don't have jobs badly want them. They are anxious, as Zach's father was, to be self-sufficient. They only need half a chance.

To me the greatest part of the news was that a steady job for his dad might give Zach some time to stabilize, build a sense of belonging in a community, and heal some of the wounds he was carrying inside.

"You know what this means?" Zach said with a huge grin. "I'll be in town a while. Maybe we could spend some time together?"

"Maybe," I responded, and gave him a big hug.

✂

Zach and I swapped phone calls frequently after he and his father left the shelter and moved into an apartment. Being a young mother myself, I had an idealistic vision of a mother's important responsibilities, and I was troubled by the fact that Zach was being raised without a mother. I felt a special bond with this child because I sensed his need to be nurtured and wanted desperately to help fill that need. I wanted to do more for him. I couldn't let go.

Zach was enrolled in public school where he was making new friends, but I knew that outside of school hours, he was alone a great deal of the time and had little to do. To me, the easiest solution seemed to be inviting him along with the family when we were able to get extra basketball tickets or to go roller skating. The friendship between Zach and my own children was instant, and they were happy when we included him in family activities. But this was only the beginning.

One day the phone rang. It was Zach. "I'm going to be alone this weekend. Could I sleep over?" he asked.

This was hardly the typical teacher-student relationship—but Zach wasn't my student anymore, I reasoned, and this was different. I consulted with Greg, and we made plans for Zach to be dropped off at our home at four o'clock on a Friday to stay over until Sunday afternoon. On Friday, Brandon and Nichole, then four and eight, were glued to the window, waiting for the first signs of Zach's arrival.

"When's he coming?" little Brandon wanted to know.

"Soon. You have to be patient," Nichole said. Amused with the children's talk, I watched until the blue Volkswagen pulled up in front and Zach leaped out.

The children ran down the stairs, pushing one another aside, trying to get to the door first.

"Put your sleeping bag here," Brandon ordered, wanting to get all the business out of the way so he could play. They tossed Zach's belongings down the stairs into the family room.

"Can you teach me to ride bikes first?" Brandon asked excitedly. He had just inherited a red bike with training wheels. I stood in the doorway and smiled, watching as Zach eased into his role as a member of the family.

Brandon had been wanting a big brother for a long time, and after Zach played the part on that first visit, Brandon wasn't about to let him go. So, we had many sleepovers at our house. Brandon and Nichole were always excited to have Zach come and play catch or board games or just read together snuggled on the couch.

One morning after Zach had left, Nichole and Brandon asked if we could adopt him.

"He needs a family," they pleaded.

"He has a family," I reminded them. "He has a dad who loves him very much."

This didn't satisfy the kids, but we settled on allowing Zach to stay with us whenever he needed to and including him in family activities. Our little family helped fill a very important void in Zach's life. He wanted to be nurtured by a female, looked up to by brothers and sisters, and, most important, experience the completeness of an intact and stable family.

"You're lucky," I heard him say to the kids one night. "You don't have to move all the time, and both your mom and dad are here with you. You have a lot."

✂️

May of my second year at the school, I was encouraged by the progress I was seeing and happy to be in a bigger, new facility. But trying to make certain we had covered all the material the students would need to progress to their next grade had buried me alive. By 5:00 P.M. each day, I could hardly hold my eyes open to drive home. Keeping my head above water and meeting my family's needs were all I could focus on.

I didn't even notice that Zach hadn't been in touch.

Just as I was preparing to leave school one day, the telephone rang. I decided to ignore it, but after six rings, I felt edgy. "What if it's my kids?" I thought. I picked up the phone to hear John, at the front desk, say, "You have visitors down here."

I sighed. No doubt people from the community looking for a service project for their group. Of course we wanted their help, but I was tired. "I'm so tired, John. Could you handle it?"

"Stacey, it's Zach and Jim."

I responded quickly, "I'll be right down."

I gathered the papers I still had to correct and my jacket, glancing over the room which was a shambles after six hours with twenty-five kids who wanted to be outside where it was spring. At the bottom of the stairs, though, all the worries fled as I was greeted by two happy, familiar smiles.

"Good news, Stace," Zach's father beamed happily. "I got myself a new job in Alaska. You know, there's good money there and good schools."

As I stepped off the last stair, I turned to Zach. "Well, what do you think about that idea?" I asked him.

"Fine, fine, it sounds kinda fun," Zach said. I knew him well enough to see behind what he was saying. The loss was about to begin again. I wondered how much I could stand to watch.

Late that night I got a phone call.

"We haven't left yet," Zach said.

"Oh, good," I replied. He then proceeded to offer me his most prized possessions. I couldn't help thinking of a child who prepares himself for suicide by dispersing of all of his personal belongings.

"Zach, are you sure you want me to have these things?" I asked softly.

"Yes, I'm sure. Will you take good care of my bird?" I didn't dare let on to my true feelings. What in the world would I do with a bird?

"I promise it will be loved," I responded solemnly.

Zach delivered his treasures the next day. My son inherited several Nintendo games, and I now had a bird, which I promised to love and feed every day in Zach's honor. The good-byes were difficult, but I knew he wasn't a rookie. A few weeks after he left, a postcard arrived to let me know he was finally safe in Alaska. One night a few months later Zach gave me a special gift.

It was almost midnight. I was sound asleep when the phone rang.

"Stacey, is that you?"

"Yes," I replied, not quite sure to whom I was speaking.

"Are you watching the Whitney Houston special?"

"No, I'm not," I moaned, still not sure who was on the other end.

"She's singing 'The Greatest Love of All,' you know, the song you used to sing to us."

I cried out, recognizing Zach's voice at last, "Oh, Zach, I wish I was. How are you?"

"I'm fine, I was hoping you were watching because she reminded me of you and how you taught us to love ourselves."

I was stunned into silence.

"I just started thinking of you, and I thought maybe I'd call."

"I'm glad you did." I assured Zach that it wasn't too late to call then listened for about fifteen minutes to his tales of life in Alaska.

As I lay in bed that night after we talked, my heart was full, amazed to see that we really can make a difference in a child's life. We really can teach hope through something as simple as love. Suddenly I hadn't ever had a bad day on the job. I had never been wasting my time. I lay there believing we could save every child. I lay there thinking of Zach.

✂

I thank Stacey for giving me all the willpower and encouragement to stay in school, to think positive about myself and things like that. Now I know how important it is for me to graduate, and I know I can. I think she'll always have a place in my heart because of that. Whenever I hear the song "The Greatest Love of All" by Whitney Houston, I almost always automatically pick up the phone and give her a call even if it's real late at night. I guess I'll always do that.

✂

Calls from Zach became fewer and farther between until one night just about a year ago. My sister and her family were visiting, and I excused myself to answer the phone when it rang.

"Stacey, I haven't forgotten you. Do you remember me?

This is Zach." I hardly recognized his voice. My memories were of a child; I was now talking with a young man.

"I'm still in school, Stacey. And guess what? I'm going to graduate. I'll be the only one in my family to get a high school diploma. My brothers want me to get my GED, but I want to graduate from high school." I congratulated him and asked him to tell me everything he was doing. He was in Colorado now, and everything was fine.

"Can I come and see you?" he asked.

"Sure, of course," I replied. "When?" We worked out the details, and a week later I was sitting at the bus depot with the jitters so bad you would have thought I was a schoolgirl waiting on a first date. To top off my nerves, I was practicing my confession. We had moved the year before, and Zach's bird had gotten away. Nichole and Brandon had been outraged; they had grown to love the bird quite fiercely. I had never grown to love the bird, and I felt guilty that I hadn't felt worse about its escape. Then Zach stepped off the bus, and when our eyes met, I just broke down and cried. I wiped the tears away to get a better look as Zach waved and hurried over. He'd grown a thin, blonde mustache and though he was short, he was bigger than I was. He still wore a baseball cap, and though he looked tired from his all-night bus ride, he still carried himself with the same style and presence that I remembered when he was eleven and twelve. Now he was seventeen.

For two weeks we caught up on each other's lives. Zach had been staying with his two brothers in Colorado, brothers he hadn't seen for fourteen years. He had also been able to spend some time with his mother. He told me of the anger he still felt towards her, even after they had talked for hours about the actual circumstances of their separation. For fourteen years Zach had created a picture of a woman who was callous enough to turn away a toddler. Her explanation was quite different.

In order to receive the divorce she longed for, she had to accept certain conditions. Her husband wanted Zach. His mother agreed, thinking it would be temporary, believing that Zach's father's wandering lifestyle wouldn't permit him to keep a toddler around. However, the future would prove to be different than any of them had imagined. Even though Zach's father continued to move from place to place looking for a better life, he never considered letting go of his boy.

At home in the evenings during Zach's visit we cooked together as a family—taco salad, barbecued hamburgers. Zach kept trying to wean me off Diet Coke by offering me his all-natural Snapple.

"I don't need any of that healthy stuff," I insisted. "You look this good when you're as old as I am." We went to the batting cages, played plenty of late-night card games, and laughed a lot. Even though many changes had taken place in our home—the kids were much older and McKenzie had been born to us six months earlier—Zach still fit right in. Brandon kept Zach busy in the afternoons with baseball, and Zach was cute with the baby, snuggling her a lot and talking to her in baby talk when he figured no one else was listening.

During the days, Zach went back with me to the School With No Name to teach.

"This is weird for me to be a volunteer in a place where I used to live," he said while he wandered around the brightly lit room, peering at the bookshelves stuffed with children's books and the counters piled with student work and class pets.

"Where did you get the rabbit?" he asked, kneeling down to rub our white bunny behind the ears.

"A volunteer who was moving and thought this was a good place for the rabbit. He's smart."

"Does he just run around loose?" Zach questioned.

"She plays ball with the kids," I explained, giving the rabbit's big, pink ball a soft kick. Sandy took off across the room to retrieve it.

"This place is a lot better than the old place, but I'll bet you don't like these kids as well as you liked us," Zach teased.

"You were little monsters," I retorted. Then I said soberly, "I think a lot of the kids are different now, though." I had Zach's attention now, but I didn't know if I could explain what I felt.

"Back at the old shelter, there were a lot of people like you and your dad, people who moved around a lot and didn't settle down. There were a lot you knew had been poor, really poor, and deprived for a long time. Now we're getting people who've just lost their jobs and can't pay the rent. I think we have lots of families who come through who never imagined they would need someplace like this." I stopped myself, looking into Zach's face, knotted with thought.

Zach nodded, as the children began bustling through the door.

✀

Since I came back I've went to school with Stacey to help her kids, and it makes me feel good to see the changes that have taken place. The school's four times bigger, it's cleaner, they've got regular desks and more books. They've got paper, they've got pencils, they've got everything now. Before we didn't have anything. And I feel good because we had a couple of volunteers come in, but now they have a lot of volunteers come in, actors and all kinds of people. It's unbelievable, and it makes me feel good that I can sit down and help the kids with their math or something because I've stayed in school and I know how to do it.

✀

I kept an eye on Zach as he worked with the students. He would look up from where he was helping a second grader work with the counting blocks or from kneeling over an English worksheet at one of the low tables and grin. He helped the kids with their math, and he shared with them what he had learned from school and from life on the move with his father: *Stay in school. Believe in yourself. Love yourself.* I could see him giving back to his world what had been given to him.

✂

I think homelessness is a terrible thing. I think everybody should be off the streets. They should all have a place to be, like at home or at a job. They should all have something to do. When I was homeless it made me feel real bad as a kid because everything was gone—my dreams, my hopes, my clothes, my house. I had nowhere to go run and hide if I got mad. It was just down, and I have a feeling kids now feel the same way I did and probably even more so because more and more people are becoming homeless. And it's really sad because there are a lot of rich people out there who are just sitting on their money and don't even volunteer. They don't have to give their money—just volunteer, it would help out a lot. It would also help out the kids tremendously to buy them new shoes or something when they leave so that when they go to a regular school kids don't make fun of them. That was probably my biggest thing—kids making fun of me, saying, "Oh, huh huh, you were in the homeless shelter" and laughing at me.

✂

Too soon it was time for Zach to go back to Colorado. As we did his laundry together, late one evening, I asked him what he was going to take back with him from this trip.

"Spend lots of time with your kids and you'll be happy," he said. "And work hard."

"I'm proud of you," I told him, while I smoothed a folded t-shirt. "I hope you'll always remember that."

"I will," he promised. Then he added, "Don't forget me."

"I won't," I assured him. How could I ever forget.

✂

I've learned from homelessness that it can happen to anybody. I didn't think it would happen to me but it did. I think the schools should give kids lessons, tours, field trips, like overnight stays in a homeless shelter just so everybody in the world will realize what homelessness is like. If I had one wish, I'd wish that all the people in the world had a place to live and always had food on their table and always had clothes on their backs. That would be my wish to the whole world. I'd give up my life for something like that. ✐

The Adult Population: The Unhealed Child

I was giving a tour of the shelter yesterday when an elderly woman leaned over to me and whispered, "Doesn't this disgust you? You know, all the lazy people standing outside your classroom window who don't want to work?"

I politely said, "No, it just makes me sad." I didn't let on how furious I felt; I remembered my first days at the shelter, before I knew these people. Still, all the way home I kept chiding myself. "Why didn't you take the time to teach her? Why didn't you say, 'These people are real human beings with personalities, with hopes, dreams, and fears. These people are our brothers and sisters.'" Her naive question upset me so much that when I went to speak to a large audience that night I scrapped my well-known child advocacy presentation and spoke for two hours about the adult homeless population.

To me, my students' parents, the guests at the women's shelter, the men wandering the streets are not faceless people. They are not numbers to be counted as a statistic indicating how bad homelessness is getting. They are people. People with immense empathy and compassion. People who hunger for a better life just as we all do. People who often haven't had a childhood that provided self-esteem or self-worth. People like Jim. . .

✂

"Another day, so few dollars," I joked out loud as I passed the familiar faces that greeted me along my daily walk through the streets to the men's shelter and then into my classroom. I chose this path because I needed a better understanding of what kept haunting me as I drove away to the security of my own beautiful home: the images of scores of adults standing outside the shelter with looks of hopelessness worn on their weary faces. I needed to know them.

"How do they feel?" I wondered. "What do they hope for? What do they have to teach me about homelessness?" I felt strongly that not enough was being done, but I didn't know what they really needed until one day I learned a valuable lesson from a wise old man who had lived on the streets for years. We became pals one morning as I cheerfully joked with the guys gathered outside the shelter about being just crazy enough to keep coming back year after year.

"It isn't the money," I complained. "I pay more in taxes than I actually take home." From where he sat on the sidewalk, an old man looked up with tired eyes.

"You're not here for the dollars," he said. "I've watched you. I seen you light up when the kids yell out to you before you even get out of your car."

"You're a wise man," I said, studying the old man on the sidewalk. His face was burnt the brown of an old leather glove, and wisps of his gray hair floated like corn silk. "The children nourish me as much as I nurture them. It's a pretty good trade."

Then he spoke words that imprinted on my mind forever, "I wish someone would have inspired me like that when I was a kid; who knows, maybe I wouldn't be on the streets today."

"I wish someone would have," I thought out loud. There was a child inside of him who had never been reached. Is that what causes homelessness, I wondered? Does it start so far back, with things that happened long ago?

I appreciated this heartfelt wisdom, and the next morning I stopped by the shelter desk to inquire about this man. He hadn't given me his name, so I wasn't sure if the men's shelter staff would know who I was talking about. To my surprise, all I needed to do was describe him and they knew immediately who I meant.

"His name is Jim. He was lookin' for you," said one staff member.

"Me?" I said.

"Yeah," he responded, rifling through a pile of notes on the desk. "He had a gift for you." The staff member picked up an intercom microphone and blared out through the building: "Jim, the old school marm is here to see you."

In a few moments, Jim came barreling through the door like a child on Christmas morning. As he caught his breath, he presented me with a gray and rose colored quilt.

"This is for you," he said beaming from ear to ear. "It's too nice to use out on the streets, and that's where I usually sleep."

"It's beautiful."

"It's the only really nice thing I own, but I haven't really got no use for it," Jim admitted.

"I can't take it," I insisted.

"Sure you can take it. I already told you, I don't use it. You can wrap up in it at night. It'll remind you of the people at the shelter."

That night I cuddled up on the couch with the quilt wrapped around me. My son Brandon asked where it came from, and I told him of my encounter with Jim and what Jim had taught me. Intrigue filled Brandon's eyes as I told him about the adults at the shelter.

"You know, Brandon," I said, as he curled up underneath the quilt with me, "somebody didn't take the time to tell Jim that he was important. Somebody missed the chance to love him through a lonely childhood, so he turned to alcohol to soothe his pain." In Jim's honor we named the quilt *The Love Quilt*. We tried to treat it the same way we hope we would have treated Jim if we had been lucky enough to have known him as a child. Each night we snuggled up in it and remembered what this priceless gift symbolized. I learned a very simple lesson that day. We never know who is watching; we never know when what we have to give might meet another's need. No matter how simple the act may seem, we may never get another opportunity to touch someone's life.

✂

Sarah was the woman who waited with me for McKenzie to be born. I could hear her cussing out the guys gathered on the sidewalk every morning as I walked into the shelter. Men would move out of her way to save themselves from tackling her head-on. I trembled myself sometimes as I heard her scold the men who hassled her. She was crude and crass, loud enough to be heard in the next county, and enough of a bully to have taken care of herself for years on the streets.

Sarah and I had our first encounter on a cold, snowy day. She walked into the shelter looking for a coat. I could hear her from the desk. Her abrasiveness didn't get her very far, but I couldn't help thinking that maybe Sarah didn't know any better. Maybe Sarah had to demand in order to get by. Maybe it was a skill she developed from childhood in order to survive. The family shelter couldn't give her a coat in any case because the donations were strictly for the guests living there, but I couldn't bear it. I ran after Sarah and caught her at the double glass doors leading outside.

"Sarah, is that your name?" I asked, panic filling my body. "I'm the school teacher. I think I have a coat for you." Sarah followed me to the classroom without saying a word. She tried on the coat, and for the first time I saw a beautiful smile cross her face. With it came a softness that had been tucked way down inside so that no one could see her vulnerability.

"Thank you," she said.

"You're very welcome, and by the way, you look beautiful," I replied while I reached out to turn down the collar. The coat was white and furry, very warm and feminine. For the first time in a long time Sarah caught a little good feeling floating in the air.

From then on, it seemed that every morning Sarah would

greet me on the streets with a warm smile. When I was feeling down or questioning why I came to work in this stressful environment, my answer would be staring at me on Sarah's face. People need people regardless of their circumstances. I loved Sarah and understood her style—I had learned that the attitude considered necessary to survive on the streets was "you had better get them before they get you."

It was a cold day in December when I found out in the medical clinic at work that I was pregnant with McKenzie. I walked out of the shelter with tears running down my cheeks and a wide smile on my face.

"Stacey," Sarah yelled from across the street, "are you all right?"

"Sarah, I'm going to have a baby," I shouted back. Sarah came over, felt my tummy, and looked at me with a frown.

"Does this mean you're gonna quit?"

"Oh, Sarah," I said, unable to think clearly from the excitement, "I don't think I could leave this place." Later, as I was driving home, Sarah's words came back to me and struck panic in my heart. What would I do? My job, the children who counted on me every day, the kids who repeated at the school, continuing in the cycle of homelessness—I needed to be there. But what about my baby? They were questions that would go on troubling me until the day I bundled up my new little girl and trundled her off to school with me.

As the weeks progressed, I became more and more nauseous with my pregnancy. Quitting didn't seem like such a bad idea anymore. On one particularly bad day I passed Sarah on the sidewalk. Sarah looked distressed and in pain.

"What's up, Sarah? Are you OK?"

"I'm OK." I knew she wasn't OK, so I knelt down beside her. Her pant leg was pulled up, revealing a cluster of open sores. She was trying to apply some medication to them.

"My arthritis is so bad today that it hurts to bend," Sarah moaned. I knew she needed help with this, but I didn't want to help, and I wasn't sure if I could do it anyway without throwing up. Being pregnant and nauseated was not good for taking care of open sores. I held my breath, said a prayer, and proceeded to help her with the ointment. I forced myself to control my queasy stomach until she was out of sight—then I vomited.

Together, Sarah and I watched the baby grow. My tummy grew larger and larger, and I became more and more tired. Sarah would ask me daily how many more days until the final countdown. On August 12, I was frantically preparing materials for my substitute late into the night. The baby was to be induced the next day. Sarah saw the light on and peeked into the stifling classroom.

"What are you doing here, Stacey?"

"I'm going to have my baby tomorrow and there's so much to do. I'm a little scared," I confessed. Sarah and I shared a quiet moment while I watched her from across the table where my work lay spread out.

"I'll pray for you," Sarah determined finally.

"Thanks, Sarah, I'll let you know how things work out." Our beautiful baby girl was born to us the next day. By October I was expected back to work, and that was when I decided that my baby girl would be with me. The people on the streets had been good to me, and I knew they would love this beautiful child.

Sarah was the first to greet us, and she cradled little McKenzie in her arms like a pro. She was a pro. Sarah had given birth to five children in her younger years but all five had been taken from her. I wanted so badly to talk, but I sensed that it wasn't the time. So I stood and watched Sarah, wrapped in the white coat from last winter, now a dingy gray. Sarah, the holy terror of the streets around the shelter. Sarah who stood now amidst the men on the sidewalk, cooing over this baby at her neck like a young girl. Sometimes we need to let down our guard, throw out the rules, and cuddle up to people. Like Zach said, "If everyone would just take one person and love them, imagine how much better our world would be."

✄

It is too easy to dismiss homelessness and the homeless as a result of alcohol or drug abuse. Many of the parents of the children I have written about have problems with substance abuse, but I have just as many children whose parents don't. Of those who do, I don't know how many had a serious problem before they ended up on the streets and how many have turned to alcohol and drugs in trying to deal with their troubles. Today, lack of education plays an increasing role in homelessness, as does the availability of affordable housing. Trying to find someplace for a family to live on a five-dollar-an-hour job in a city with an apartment vacancy rate of 2% can be nearly impossible. Domestic violence, too, is driving women to the streets in increasing numbers, often with their children.

I pulled up to the shelter just before nine o'clock one cold morning and noticed one of my students and her mother waiting patiently for my arrival.

"I'm glad you're here," Mrs. Allen, the mother, said, looking worried. "I can't leave Amanda here alone with all these crazy people. I have an appointment at Welfare Square in an hour and I need to go." With a practiced smile, she turned to coax her toddlers into keeping up with the stroller.

"We have a long walk, boys, so keep up with me," Mrs. Allen said. Three pairs of big, blue, tired eyes looked up at her.

"I'm cold," four-year-old Isaiah said. That was enough for me. It would only take minutes to drive them. Fishing out my keys for Mrs. Allen, I pointed to the blue Bronco in the parking lot.

"Go get in, I'll be right back," I said. I stopped by the classroom long enough to put my students in the care of my teaching assistant and ran back to the car. As I climbed in I noticed that the two little boys were not wearing socks inside of their boots.

"Why don't you have socks on, Isaiah?" I asked.

"We didn't pack any," he said sadly. "We left in the night so Dad wouldn't hurt us no more." We were quiet for the rest of the trip. I am sure Mrs. Allen was embarrassed, and I just couldn't find anything to say.

I had heard Mrs. Allen's stories of the beatings she took from her husband, stories that left my stomach sick. Knowing that simply hearing of the brutality made me feel like vomiting, I can't imagine the price she paid for so many years. She finally found the courage to pack her old, beat-up car with a few of the kids' things, take off one night, and never look back. After crossing several state lines into safety, the car died, leaving them no transportation once they got to Salt Lake City. Now Mrs. Allen is a single mother with five children. No car, no money, no friends or family here. But she is determined in her quest for a better life, and she is a good mother to her children.

✂

Though many of them need help, the adults I meet are hardly helpless victims with nothing to offer. Late one afternoon, I was in my room trying to draw a castle to use in presenting a writing idea to my students the next morning. Zero artistic talent didn't help my already frustrated efforts. I let out an exasperated howl and flipped my pencil across the room, which brought the night janitor on the run.

"You OK?" he said with a look of horror on his face.

"Sorry," I said sheepishly. "I need a castle for a lesson tomorrow, but I just can't draw." The janitor left his mop and bucket in the middle of the floor and came back in a few minutes towing an old man by the elbow.

"This is Steve," the janitor said. "He's an artist. He can draw whatever you need."

Hesitantly, Steve took the chair next to mine. He puckered his brow into a perplexed knot as he studied my handiwork. Then he looked up at me.

"It's a castle, and don't you dare say you didn't know that," I warned him.

Steve grinned from ear to ear, picked up a pencil from the table, and turned my posterboard over.

"*This* is a castle," he informed me. In quick, measured strokes, he began to sketch. While I watched over his shoulder, walls, a drawbridge, and towers appeared on the paper as though Steve were only uncovering what had already been there. His breathing grew labored while he worked, as though this were a taxing effort. He finished with a fair maiden peering out a window atop the castle's highest tower.

"That's you," he panted as he straightened up, "trapped inside with all those kids, and you can't get out."

We both laughed, and I took a closer look at Steve. He must have been my grandfather's age, almost bald, short, and husky.

"How did you learn to draw castles like that?" I asked.

"It's a gift," he said, smiling. "It doesn't hurt that I've been wishing I had a castle of my own. Hell, a shack would be a castle to me right now."

As Steve left, I looked at the castle and thought about how he needed to have an outlet for his art and how I needed help. I was teaching all seven grades with the assistance of just one teaching aide. I wondered if Steve and I could strike some sort of a deal that would help us both. Maybe I could pay him to make some props for lessons.

The next day when my boss dropped by to see how things were going. I showed Steve's castle to him and told him how I wished I could use him to do more projects for the class. Luck must have been on Steve's side, too, because at that moment he walked through the door just beaming to show off some things he had been up the night before creating for me to use in teaching my classes. There were cartoon characters that taught measurements, parts-of-speech posters that rhymed, animal pictures to stir up writing ideas. My favorite was a chimpanzee with a stalk of wheat in his mouth with the words "I Love You Because ____" written across the bottom. Steve was breathing heavily again, and I thought he was just excited about showing his work.

"Calm down," I joked. "The drawings are great."

"That's just my emphysema," he wheezed. "You really like them?"

"Yup," I said. "I want to use them all." After Steve left, I turned to my boss to beg.

"Can't I hire him to help me?" I pleaded. My boss nodded his head and smiled. This was a man I always had admired, a man who saw a need and acted.

"Let's set him up," he said.

Steve came on as my artist, secretary, organizational expert, and general sounding board. For the next four months, including the time that Tucker spent at the school, Steve kept the classroom in tip-top shape. He was a master of "a place for everything and everything in its place." I was his challenge, with my own preferred filing system of letting things stay where they landed. Together, with his visual aids, we taught everything from music to grammar. The kids loved learning with his creations, and I grew to count on and love him like a second grandfather.

Steve was a wanderer, as some of the homeless have always been. I didn't know his reasons. He certainly wasn't lazy—I still pull out a lesson every now and again neatly labeled and realistically illustrated by Steve. He was dying of emphysema, but it didn't stop him from moving on or sharing with us before he left. I knew he would go someday, just as all my students did, but I didn't know how much it would affect me. I can still look at his castle or one of his lessons, and it brings back a flood of warm memories. It brings back a person who was full of talents and gifts, someone who met my needs at a time when I couldn't meet them by myself.

✄

Finally, I have to give you one more look at my friend Sarah. Each time I walk past the pudding aisle in the grocery store, I have to smile to myself, remembering one of the last encounters we had before the school year ended. I had made a five-dollar bet with one of my students that he couldn't get five perfect scores in a row on his spelling tests. Obviously, I lost because I was making a mad rush to my car through the pouring rain to retrieve a five-dollar bill. With the bill tucked in my pocket, I raced back to the red-brick building, barely able to spot the green door through the pounding rain. From the corner of my eye, I caught sight of a large, furry figure crouched against the building and making sobbing noises.

"Sarah, is that you?" I hollered, as I darted over to investigate. Sarah looked at me with the yearning eyes of a child.

"I'm cold, and I'm hungry," she cried, never one to mince words, as she sloshed over and fell into me in a soaking bear hug.

"Come in, and we'll find you something to eat," I coaxed, completely drenched by now.

All eyes stared as I escorted Sarah through the back door. I could make out the whispers being passed among the children, "That's Sarah, she's the one who yells a lot." I sat Sarah in the rocking chair, slipped off her soggy, gray coat, and began reciting our list of snacks.

"We have applesauce, crackers, raisins, juice." The children were smiling now as they understood what was going on. Sarah was wiping her eyes and face as she warmed up to the security of the classroom.

"I want chocolate pudding," she belted out. I hadn't even spotted it in the cupboard, but she had. I handed her one of the little cups, then went to find her a spoon.

"Teacher, look," Matthew whispered as I walked past. Sarah had already dug into the pudding with her index finger. It was gone in an instant, and she was asking for more before I ever found her something to eat with.

The kids and I brainstormed together on where we might find some sweats large enough for Sarah, and after a couple of in-house phone calls we came up with some dry clothes. Meanwhile, Sarah made herself comfortable in our big rocking chair with the baby doll that Marissa, a kindergartner, had placed in her lap.

Sarah spent the rest of the afternoon tipping back and forth in that chair. Every once in a while I'd make eye contact and smile as I moved among the children. Sarah seemed content to sit and rock her doll. She was as quiet and content as I had ever seen her. When the last of the children left that afternoon, I packed a bag of snacks for Sarah to have for dinner and loaded her and the food into my car.

The rain was still coming down in sheets as we made our way through the streets to find her hotel room. I didn't know who had put her up in a room or why she hadn't spent the day there, but I didn't ask. I was just grateful she had someplace to go. Sarah stayed quiet in the car, telling me only to turn here or there as I struggled to make out street signs. When we pulled up to the curb, I jumped out and ran around to the other side of the car to help her out. Sarah didn't move.

"Come on, Sarah, let's go," I said, forcing a smile while the cold rain trickled down my neck. "I've got to get home to my baby." Reluctantly, Sarah heaved herself out of the car, splashing right through the flooding gutter, and followed me to her door. As I worked the key into the lock, I noticed that Sarah was leaning heavily against the door jamb.

"We better put you right to bed," I joked. For what might have been the first time since I had known her, she didn't argue, and I worried that she might be seriously ill. Her gray hair hung on her face in plastered strings. When I got the door open, the room wasn't much bigger than the single bed along one wall. There was a small bureau at the head of the bed and one chair.

"Come on," I urged, motioning Sarah over to the bed.

I set the snacks close to her bed where she wouldn't have to get up to eat them and tugged her shoes off her swollen feet while Sarah whined softly.

"Now lay down and rest," I said, patting Sarah gently. The room was dark with afternoon shadows from the gray day, and from outside I could hear the sound of cars swishing by on the wet pavement. Sarah stopped whimpering and lay back in the bed. The faint red letters on a small clock radio by her bed read 4:35. I had an hour's work left back at the school before I could go home to my own children. Sarah rolled over and sighed.

"Is everything OK?" I asked, bending down to look at her. I could smell the musty scent of Sarah's heavy blanket, and a big tear rolled down her left cheek.

"I love you," Sarah whispered, half asleep and smiling.

"I love you, too," I said, then sat on the bed to wait for her to fall asleep. ✎

A Simple Answer to a
Complex Problem: Serve

One morning at the School With No Name, the kids and I were discussing the importance of friendship. We were comparing the difference between put-ups and put-downs and the effect they have on us. The children expressed concern that what they hear may impact who they become. "I think you're right," I told them, "So shouldn't we carefully choose what comes out of our mouths so we don't destroy another child's self-esteem? Shouldn't we show people we love them by the things that we say?" Curtis, a charming but troubled young man, spoke matter-of-factly, as though he were an expert on the power of words.

"You know, teacher, *nobody don't love nobody,*" he said.

That haunting phrase would not leave my mind. I couldn't figure out where I had heard those words before until one night at the dinner table my grandfather started telling stories.

He began, "You know, when Stacey was a little girl she was obsessed with making sure that everyone was treated fairly. When things didn't run smoothly she would stand at the bottom of the stairs with her big brown eyes filled with tears and cry out, "Grandpa, *nobody don't love nobody.*"

One tragic lesson I have learned from the children at the School With No Name is that we are destroying each other everywhere. I came to know the children in this book because they came through the shelter where I work, but there is no shortage of tragedy, physical and emotional devastation, and deprivation in middle- and upper-class homes. The most serious deprivation any child—any person—faces is not financial. It is the deprivation of experience, the deprivation of opportunity, and too often it is the deprivation of self, through lack of love and positive or stable experience.

I hope that you have allowed yourself to live for a few moments in the tattered shoes of some of my students. I know that these stories take people out of their comfort zone, but I don't share these stories to make others feel guilty or hopeless. I tell you these stories in an attempt to inspire you to act. On behalf of all of the children who have passed through the *School With No Name* I want you to also feel hopeful that through love and service the world could be a kinder place. A child is waiting to hear that he or she is a valued part of your community. You might be surprised, if kids find appropriate feelings of belonging and power, we won't have to fear them in large gangs. And, of course, the need extends beyond childhood. We live surrounded by the poor, the lonely, the hungry, the abused—the needy. They are our family and neighbors, they are strangers and friends. There is a particular satisfaction one gets from reaching out to meet the needs of another, a certain peace and pleasure that comes with giving. I've heard about it from the volunteers who help at the school, and I have felt it myself.

The following pages present some great places to start, ways anybody can get in and make a difference. It's up to you how you serve; there are as many different ways as there are needs, time, resources, and talents. Don't be overwhelmed by all that needs to be done. The important thing is to do *something*. It simply takes making an effort to prove Curtis wrong, to prove that *somebody does love somebody.*

At Home

When looking for what needs to be done and somebody to love and serve, don't forget those around you. If we begin by taking care of our own families and neighbors, we help keep intact those important social networks which keep people functioning even through hard times.

- Becoming a foster parent—you can get information from the Division of Family Services in your phone book.
- Big Brothers or Big Sisters—you can find them in a phone book.
- Prepare Christmas or Thanksgiving meals, etc. for families who are struggling.
- Adopt a grandparent—you can get information from the Department of Human Services in your phone book.
- Be a foster grandparent.
- Take someone to a doctor's appointment.
- Join the PTA.
- Coach a little league team or be a team mom.
- Volunteer at your children's school.
- Volunteer at a neighborhood school as a tutor.
- Get to know a neighbor—make a double batch of something to share or just go over and say hello.
- Call a relative or friend you haven't talked to for a while.
- Visit a nursing home—don't forget your own relatives.
- Baby-sit for a tired parent.
- Write an overdue letter.
- Get involved with your children's scout troop.
- Give some special attention to a child or grandchild who might be struggling.

In Town

For service to your community, the telephone book can be your most valuable resource for getting started. Once you start asking questions about volunteer work, you might be amazed at the variety of needs and oportunities surrounding you.

☞ **Human Services.** In the blue state government pages of your telephone book under Human Services you should be able to find a phone number for a Volunteer Services coordinator. Departments and services under Human Services include: Aging Services, Child Abuse and Neglect Services, Family Services, Handicapped Services, Mental Health, Youth Corrections. These and other departments can use volunteers in both "person-to-person" and technical areas.

☞ Companies can adopt families or schools.

☞ Volunteer at a homeless shelter or soup kitchen.

☞ Donate to or volunteer at a food bank.

☞ Volunteer at a local children's hospital, general hospital, or burn center.

☞ Contact your local library to volunteer for literacy programs or to read to the blind or children.

☞ Child abuse prevention programs—you might check with Human Services to see what is being done in your area.

☞ Volunteer at a crisis center or hotline—Human Services might be able to give you a lead.

☞ Join a service-oriented club like the Kiwanis, Lions, Rotary International, or Jaycees.

☞ Run for local office.

☞ Volunteer to help with a program for teenage mothers—maybe even throw a young mother a baby shower.

- Participate in fundraisers benefitting groups or causes you are interested in.
- Donate clothing to the Salvation Army, a shelter, or a thrift store.
- Serve through your local church.

In Your State, Nation, and the World

Again, once you begin looking, the needs and opportunities for service are almost endless. The short list that follows is only a beginning. Many of these agencies act as clearinghouses to direct people to a number of different types of specific programs. You may also want to pick a favorite charity and make a regular donation.

Volunteers of America
National Office
3939 North Causeway Blvd.
Matairie, LA 70002
1-800-899-0089

Founded in 1896, Volunteers of America is one of the largest and most diversified non-profit human services agencies in the United States. They offer more than 400 programs that extend help to youth, the elderly, families in crisis, abused and neglected children, the homeless, people with disabilities, and ex-offenders returning to society. Their goal is to provide opportunities for people to express their deepest faith by serving others.

American Red Cross
National Headquarters
17th and D Streets, N.W.
Washington, D.C. 20006

The American Red Cross has over 2000 offices in the United States, which provide a wide range of services. Contact your local American Red Cross office and ask for the Office of Volunteer Personnel.

Points of Light Foundation
1-800-879-5400

The Points of Light Foundation coordinates numerous volunteer efforts across the country. When you call, they will direct you to one of the local volunteer centers in your area or provide you with a list of other alternatives if they do not have a center near you.

Habitat for Humanity
1-800-HABITAT

Habitat for Humanity is an international organization that builds and renovates housing for low income people.

The National Resource Center on Homelessness and Mental Illness
262 Delaware Ave.
Delmar, NY 12054
1-800-444-7415

A national organization concerned with mental health, housing, and homelessness. A resource center for people who want to learn more about homelessness.

Youth Service America
1101 15th Street North West
Suite 200
Washington, D.C. 20005

Write for a brochure to find out how you can get involved in your own community.

Travelers Aid International
512 C Street North East
Washington, D. C. 20002
202-546-3120

Travelers Aid International (TAI) is a network of local agencies that provides information and assistance to thousands of travelers, homeless people, runaway youth, and others. TAI agencies provide shelter, transitional housing programs, counseling, and other services. You can write or phone for ideas on what you can do in your area.

The Corporation for National and Community Service
1-800-942-2677
1-800-833-3772 (hearing impaired)

The Corporation for National and Community Service acts as an umbrella for a number of federal service agencies, including AmeriCorps (the new national service program created by Congress and President Clinton, open to adults 18 yrs. and older who want to commit to eleven months of service), VISTA, the National Civilian Community Corps, Learn and Serve, and the Senior Corps (which includes the Foster Grandparent, Senior Companion, and the Retired and Senior and Volunteer Programs).

Youth Volunteer Corps of America
6310 Lamar Ave. Suite 145
Overland Park, KS 66202-4247
913-432-9822

The Youth Volunteer Corps promotes civic responsibility through volunteerism among youth, ages 11-18. The program draws young people from diverse ethnic and socio-economic backgrounds and actively involves them in community problem-solving through structured volunteer service. YVCs run both school-year and intensive summer service programs. YVCs may be sponsored by diverse local agencies such as YMCA, Boys and Girls Clubs, United Way, or Volunteer Centers. Call or write for information about starting a YVC in your community. ⬅

About the Author

Stacey Bess began to record the stories of some of her students at the School With No Name not because she intended to publish a book, but because the lessons were so profound. Stacey is firmly committed to teaching children their worth and helping them to recognize and use their personal power. The children she has touched, who were often labeled as unteachable in the public schools, are living proof that her methods work.

Stacey has a bachelor's degree in elementary education from the University of Utah. Her outstanding service has been recognized with a number of honors, including the Golden Deeds Award for dedication to homeless youth in 1992, the Utah Children Award for Outstanding Service to Children in 1991, and the Creative Community Leadership Award given by the University of Utah in 1993.

Stacey and her husband, Greg, have been married for fourteen years and have three children. In conjunction with her work at the School With No Name, she continues to be a leading advocate for the educational rights of impoverished children.